The American Indian

THE LEWIS HENRY MORGAN LECTURES / 1964

The University of Rochester

Rochester, New York

The American Indian

PERSPECTIVES FOR THE STUDY OF SOCIAL CHANGE

BY FRED EGGAN

CAMBRIDGE UNIVERSITY PRESS

Cambridge

London   New York   New Rochelle

Melbourne   Sydney

Published by the Press Syndicate of the University of Cambridge
The Pitt Building, Trumpington Street, Cambridge CB2 1RP
32 East 57th Street, New York, NY 10022, USA
296 Beaconsfield Parade, Middle Park, Melbourne 3206, Australia

Hard-cover edition first published in the United States by Aldine
Publishing Company, 1966.
First paperback edition published by the Cambridge University Press,
1980.

Designed by David Miller
Printed in the United States of America

Library of Congress Catalog Card Number: 80-67926
ISBN 0 521 23752 1 hardcovers
ISBN 0 521 28210 1 paperback

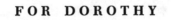

FOR DOROTHY

FOREWORD

LEWIS HENRY MORGAN WAS ASSOCIATED WITH THE UNIVERSITY of Rochester from its founding. At his death he left it his manuscripts and library, and money to found a women's college. Save for a wing of the present Women's Residence Halls that is named for him, he remained without a memorial at the University until the Lewis Henry Morgan Lectures were begun.

These Lectures owe their existence to a happy combination of circumstances. In 1961 the Joseph R. and Joseph C. Wilson families made a gift to the University, to be used in part for the Social Sciences. Professor Bernard S. Cohn, at that time Chairman of the Department of Anthropology and Sociology, suggested that establishing the Lectures would constitute a fitting memorial to a great anthropologist and would be an appropriate use for part of this gift. He was supported and assisted by Dean (later Provost) McCrea Hazlett, Dean Arnold Ravin and Associate Dean R. J. Kaufmann. The details of the Lectures were worked out by Professor Cohn and the members of his Department.

The Morgan Lectures were planned initially as three annual series, for 1963, 1964 and 1965, to be continued if circumstances permitted. It was thought fitting at the outset to have each series focussed on a particularly significant aspect of Morgan's work. Accordingly, Professor Meyer Fortes' 1963 Lectures were on kinship, Professor Fred Eggan devoted his attention to the American Indian, and Professor Robert M. Adams considered the development of civilization. The first three series were inaugurated by Professor Leslie A. White, of the University of Michigan, who delivered two lectures on Morgan's life and work in January, 1963.

Publication of Professor Eggan's Lectures makes them available to a wider public. What cannot be put between covers is a record of the pleasures and benefits enjoyed by the students and faculty of the Anthropology Department in their contacts with Professor and Mrs. Eggan during their stay at Rochester.

The present volume is a revision of the second series, delivered by Professor Eggan under the title, "Lewis H. Morgan and the American Indian," on April 7 - 21, 1964.

ALFRED HARRIS,
Department of Anthropology,
The University of Rochester

PREFACE

THE INVITATION TO PRESENT THE SECOND OF A SERIES OF
lectures at the University of Rochester honoring the contributions of Lewis Henry Morgan to the disciplines of
anthropology was a welcome one for several reasons. The
new Department of Social Anthropology at the University
is the first in the country dedicated to this important discipline, and its staff is currently engaged in developing an
exciting graduate curriculum. I have long been an ad-
mirer of Morgan's pioneer contributions to the study of
social organization, one of the central concerns of modern
social anthropology, and therefore took this occasion as an
opportunity to summarize my views on Morgan's researches on the American Indian and to bring together
my own ideas, scattered in a number of papers and monographs, as to what we have learned about social structure
and social change with reference to a number of Indian
tribes and regions. And Lewis H. Morgan himself, though
never officially connected with the University of Rochester,
was a strong supporter of this institution in its early days
and left his manuscripts to the University library, along
with an endowment for the education of women.

Professor Meyer Fortes, of Cambridge University, who
presented the first of the series of Morgan Lectures, ad-

dressed himself to the general topic of "Kinship and the Social Order." For my own contribution I have chosen the subject of "Lewis H. Morgan and the American Indian." My colleague, Professor Robert M. Adams, director of the Oriental Institute of the University of Chicago, will continue with the question of the development of civilization and the state, a major interest of Morgan in his later years. These three series should provide a modern appraisal of Morgan's scientific achievements in the field of anthropology and a more adequate basis for evaluating his position in the intellectual life of our nation.

My own contribution has been made considerably easier by the recent publication of *Lewis Henry Morgan: The Indian Journals, 1859–62* by the University of Michigan Press. These journals, edited with an introduction by Leslie A. White (1959), cover Morgan's four expeditions to the Missouri River regions of the West during successive summers and include a wealth of observations, not only on Indian society and culture on the newly established reservations, but on frontier conditions, as well. Professor White's introduction entitled "Lewis Henry Morgan: His Life and His Researches" is the outline of what we all hope will be a definitive scientific biography.

In the meantime Carl Resek, a young historian who received his Ph.D. from the University of Rochester, has published *Lewis Henry Morgan: American Scholar* (University of Chicago Press, 1960), which has greatly clarified Morgan's position in intellectual history. From Resek's researches we discover the sources of many of Morgan's basic ideas on the origins of the classificatory system and the evolution of the family, as well as the reasons for the long delay in the publication of *Systems of Consanguinity and Affinity of the Human Family* (1871).

In preparing these lectures for publication I have expanded them here and there and have added additional documentation when necessary. Together they summarize much of what I have learned with regard to American Indian social organization, both from my own research and from that of students and colleagues at the University of Chicago and elsewhere. The full presentation of the evidence on which certain conclusions rest has not been made as yet but should be available in the near future. With the controversies surrounding Morgan's contributions to social and cultural evolution I am not here particularly concerned. But I do hope to help rescue his solid contributions to the study of American Indian social organization from the neglect that they have suffered.

During the period in April, 1964, when my wife and I were in residence at the University of Rochester, we enjoyed the privilege of living on the campus as both guests and colleagues. I would like in particular to thank President Allen Wallis, Acting Provost Robert France, and the staff of the Department of Social Anthropology, particularly Bernard Cohn, Alfred and Grace Harris, Robert Merrill, and James C. Downs, for making us welcome and looking after our comfort. A word of appreciation also for the graduate students who included us in their activities, listened with interest, and argued freely on various points.

FRED EGGAN

CONTENTS

I

LEWIS H. MORGAN AND THE
STUDY OF SOCIAL ORGANIZATION[1]

I

A MAJOR FEATURE OF THE POSTWAR PERIOD HAS BEEN THE
rise of social anthropology among the anthropological
disciplines in the United States, with a consequent emphasis upon the social system and its principles of organization and change. According to Professor Lévi-Strauss:

> The main feature of the development of social anthro-
> pology in the past years has been the increased attention to
> kinship. This is indeed not a new phenomenon, since it can
> be said that, with his *Systems of Consanguinity and Affinity of
> the Human Family*, Morgan's genius at one and the same time
> founded social anthropology and kinship studies and brought
> to the fore the basic reasons for attaching such importance to

[1] In writing this introductory chapter I have drawn freely on my
"Lewis H. Morgan in Kinship Perspective," a paper prepared for *Essays
in the Science of Culture in Honor of Leslie A. White* (ed. Gertrude E.
Dole and Robert L. Carneiro; New York: Thomas Y. Crowell Co., 1960),
summarizing some sections and incorporating others into the text. Here
will be found a fuller statement of my views as to Morgan's ideas and
procedures as well as more adequate documentation. Though I am not
an evolutionist in his use of the term, I am indebted to Leslie A. White
for intellectual stimulation and admire his forthright defense of Morgan.
  The background for the development of social organization is excellently presented by Sol Tax in "From Lafitau to Radcliffe-Brown: A
Short History of the Study of Social Organization" (1955).

the latter: permanency, systematic character, continuity of changes [1953: 539].

Almost forty years earlier, A. A. Goldenweiser, fresh from two seasons of field research among the Iroquois, paid a similar tribute to Morgan, but with certain reservations:

The credit for giving a firm foundation to the problems of social organization, and for impressing their importance upon the minds of American anthropologists, belongs indubitably to Lewis H. Morgan. He derived his early inspiration for Indian study from his life among the Seneca-Iroquois, by whom he was adopted and regarded as one of their own. His knowledge of Iroquois life and lore was as wide as it was deep, and it bore fruit in the famous "League of the Iroquois" (1851)—a work in which accurate observation and sweeping generalization, scientific sanity, and ethnological naiveté, went hand in hand. Since the appearance of that work, Morgan has been justly recognized as the co-discoverer with McLennan and Bachofen, of the maternal system of kinship organization [1915: 350].

Goldenweiser goes on to summarize Morgan's contributions to kinship studies and to social and cultural evolution and notes:

In the course of time, serious errors of fact and judgment were discovered in Morgan's work. Intensive exploration in many regions of the American area brought to light facts of social organization unknown to Morgan, or underestimated by him. Critical thinking along theoretical lines, on the general background of antievolutionary tendencies, went far to discredit the sweeping generalizations of Morgan's time [1915: 351].

These and other strictures (e.g., Swanton 1905, and Lowie 1914, 1936) have led many anthropologists to ignore or underestimate Morgan's positive contributions,

along with the discredited or outmoded evolutionary
quences. In the following pages I hope to honor Morgan
first by surveying his major contributions to the study of
kinship and social structure and then by seeing what we
have learned about the social organization of the American Indians in the century that has elapsed since his early
work. Our concern will be primarily with the regions east
of the Rocky Mountains and with particular tribes in
their regional settings: the Choctaw and their neighbors
in the Southeast, the Cheyenne and Arapaho in the Plains,
the Ojibwa and other groups in the Great Lakes region,
and the eastern and western Pueblos. There is much more
to the social organization of the American Indian (cf.
Eggan 1955: 501 ff. and Murdock 1955), but these regions
are the ones with which Morgan was primarily concerned
and where we can best evaluate and build on his contributions. I have also included a chapter reviewing Morgan's ideas with regard to the future of the American
Indian. He had a strong interest in their progress and welfare, and his firsthand view of Indian life gave him strong
convictions as to what should be done. We shall find him
a better prophet than many of his contemporaries.

II

Morgan was not the first to "discover" kinship systems—
according to Sol Tax (1955: 445), that honor belongs in
modern times to Father Lafitau, a French Jesuit missionary who described the Iroquois and Huron classifications
of consanguineal kindred as early as 1724. But when Morgan discovered, in 1858, that the Algonkian-speaking
Ojibwa on the southern shores of Lake Superior had a
pattern of grouping relatives similar to that he had earlier

recorded among the linguistically unrelated Iroquois Indians of New York State, he immediately saw the possible significance of his discovery and planned a large scale comparative study of kinship systems that was to have far-reaching and unexpected results. During the summers of 1859, 1860, 1861, and 1862, he made successive field trips to the Missouri region and beyond, retracing Lewis and Clark's epoch-making journey of a half-century earlier and visiting the newly established reservations and mission stations on which surviving remnants of eastern Indian tribes and those of the Prairie Plains were being settled. Beyond were the still wild tribes of the High Plains who would not be subdued until the extermination of the buffalo and the defeat of Sitting Bull.

These field trips are significant, in retrospect, as the first expeditions organized to secure data to answer specific anthropological questions. From his earlier study of the Iroquois Indians, Morgan had become acquainted with their clan and phratry organization and with the structure of their famous league or confederation. Discovering that their "classificatory" kinship system and clan organization were widespread, the Iroquois system became the "model" for the American Indian everywhere. Originally, Morgan was interested in a historical question: the origin of the American Indian, which he believed to be in Asia. He hoped to demonstrate this relationship by comparing the patterns of grouping relatives, and he thought he had succeeded when he found that the Tamils of southern India had almost exactly the same pattern of kinship as did the Iroquois. But in the meantime he had also discovered that certain Polynesian systems were even more "classificatory" than those of the Iroquois, and he was thus led to the development of his famous stages of social evolution from promiscuity, through the Malayan systems, to the American Indian clan systems, and, with the development of individual property ownership and inheritance, to the modern European systems.

While Morgan was able to enlist the support and aid of a considerable number of missionaries, government officials, and other individuals in his endeavors, he personally collected the great bulk of the kinship schedules on the American Indian that are included in *Systems*. But he did considerably more. In his *Indian Journals* (1959) he left a meticulous record of his observations on all aspects of Indian life on the prairies, as well as additional data collected from missionaries, traders, and travelers. Here he was particularly careful to distinguish what he learned from direct observation and questioning from the mass of fact and fancy that he accumulated from fellow travelers.

III

From Morgan's standpoint his great discovery with regard to kinship was the "classificatory" system of relationship, in which collateral relatives are merged with lineal relatives to give a wide extension to the system. He recognized that there was a relationship between forms of social organization and the type of kinship system, but he thought that the patterns of grouping relatives were highly stable and changed only in broad stages. Hence he came to believe that the American Indians were all at the same level, with similar patterns of social structure, for the most part. This seemed a reasonable conclusion, in that most of the groups he was able to study did have "classificatory" kinship systems. But he came too early to this conclusion and hence tended to neglect variations that turned out to be significant and to discount data that did not fit his conception of the American Indian system.

Morgan's growing conviction that the "classificatory" system of kinship was derived from a common historical source also led him to neglect alternate explanations, such as independent invention or borrowing.

Morgan's conception of kinship was likewise limited by modern standards. Despite his long contact with the Iroquois, Morgan missed an essential aspect of kinship— the day-to-day behavior patterns between relatives. He realized that kinship relations were real and basic to the political and social organization, but he never probed deeply enough to lay the foundation bare. Had he done so, he would have understood better the relations between terminology and behavior, between household and lineage, and between lineage and clan, and the history of social organization might have taken a different course, as Rivers (1914: 17) has pointed out. Yet, where his real interests were involved, as in political matters, he did probe the relations between form and practice.

Hence, despite his innovations in collecting terminological data by schedules and in the native language, Morgan was handicapped at the very start of his comparative studies. He was not conditioned by his Iroquois experience to inquire into social behavior and marriage practices in any systematic way and thus find a major part of the modern answer to the question: Why the "classificatory" system? He also faced practical difficulties in field work: informants were hard to find, and interpreters were few and far between. He discovered that women were the best informants for kinship and that often it was not possible to complete a schedule without consulting the tribal matrons.

Morgan was aware that kinship terminology was systematic, if not simple. The American Indian system, he said, "is so diversified with specializations and so complicated in its classifications as to require careful study in order to understand its structure and principles" (1871: 132). But, while he was concerned with the *similarities* that made the kinship systems "classificatory," he was not concerned to the same degree with the differences he noticed—differences that in modern perspctive give us kinship systems, such as the "Crow" and "Omaha," which are based on different principles of classification, at least in part.

Morgan's conception of kinship systems as highly stable in their patterns of grouping relatives derived from a number of sources. As linguistic phenomena he saw them partaking of the unconscious patterns of language, which were somehow transmitted "with the blood" and thus associated with the great "stocks" of mankind. And, empirically, as group after group evidenced the indicative features of the "classificatory" system, his original assumptions seemed verified, and he could dismiss the apparent exceptions that he found. Furthermore, Morgan had no baseline against which to discover and measure changes over time. He was apparently unaware of Lafitau's earlier observations on Iroquois kinship, which might have led him to the closer investigation of change, and the variant patterns he sometimes recorded were explained away as breakdowns or errors in recording.

Morgan began his examination of American Indian social systems with the Seneca as a standard for comparison. He was impressed by the Iroquois system of matrilineal exogamous clans and attempted to relate the kinship groupings to clan membership, particularly the merging of collateral with lineal kin. But the Iroquois terminological system is bilateral in character and is only partially consistent with the clan groupings. Hence, when Morgan went on to study the Siouan-speaking tribes of the Prairie and Plains regions, the Caddoans of the Prairies, and the Algonkian-speaking tribes of those areas and the Great Lakes region, he was not sensitized to variations in terminological grouping within the "classificatory" pattern that were much more consonant with lineage and clan groupings or with particular patterns of preferential marriage. And, when he discovered similar variants among the schedules he received for the Southeastern tribes, they were in such form as to prevent him from realizing the nature of the parallels and their possible significance.

Morgan did find evidence of greater divergence in the more fragmentary data on kinship terminology that he secured on Athabaskan-speaking peoples, the tribes of the Columbia River region, the Shoshone and Ute, the eastern Pueblos, and the Eskimo. The tribes of the Columbia River, in particular, showed considerable diversity, both in language and in kinship. But all these groups, in one way or another, were judged worthy of admission to the "classificatory" system, with the sole exception of the Eskimo, which in "the greater and most important fundamental characteristics of this system . . . is wanting" (1871: 277).

IV

Rivers gives Morgan full credit for his discoveries with regard to kinship:

I do not know of any discovery in the whole range of science which can be more certainly put to the credit of one man than that of the classificatory system of relationship by Lewis Morgan. By this I mean, not merely was he the first to point out clearly the existence of this mode of denoting relationship, but it was he who collected the vast mass of material, by which the essential characters of the systems were demonstrated, and it was he who was the first to recognize the great theoretical importance of his new discovery [1914: 4–5]

Rivers goes on to point out that Morgan himself was largely to blame for the rejection of the importance of this discovery by his critics, since he

was not content to demonstrate, as he might to some extent have done from his own material, the close connection between the terminology of the classificatory system, and forms of social organization. There can be little doubt that he recognized this connection, but he was not content to demonstrate the dependence of the terminology of relationship upon social forms, the existence of which was already known, or which were capable of demonstration with the material at his disposal. He passed over all these early stages of the argument and proceeded directly to refer the origin of the terminology to forms of social organization which were not known to exist anywhere in the earth and of which there was no direct evidence in the past [1914: 5–6].

Rivers' own contribution to the rehabilitation of Morgan's views, including the demonstration of the close connection between kinship terminology and certain forms of marriage and the conception of systems of relationship as a key to the history of social institutions, is well known.

I have elsewhere (1955: 519–51) discussed the significance of Rivers' contributions when applied to the social
organization of the northern Algonkians, and we will return to this problem in a later chapter. Of greater importance, however, has been the recognition that the kinship
usages of a people constitute a social system composed of
both terminology and social behavior, of which marriage
is only one aspect.

One basic reason why Morgan failed to make the most
of the materials on kinship that he collected seems to be
that he was not primarily interested in understanding
kinship systems as such but rather in using them as means
to other ends. His frames for comparison were adequate,
and he utilized linguistic and other controls, but, as the
"evidence" for the ultimate unity of the American Indians
and their derivation from Asia seemed more and more
definite, the rigor of the comparison relaxed.

We have noted that alternate explanations to derivation from a common source, such as independent invention and borrowing, were ruled out in advance, and when
Morgan returned to them it was not to test them against
new data but to emphasize the correctness of the original
assumptions. In the light of our present knowledge, we
tend to emphasize the influence of common factors in
bringing about similar social systems. Similarly, the assumption of the stability of the terminological system over
long periods was never seriously examined, though Morgan's own data on the Iroquois suggested variation over
relatively short periods. Today we would reverse Morgan's
assumptions and consider the terminological patterns as
relatively sensitive indicators of social change.

From a larger perspective Lowie has wondered what Morgan's scheme

might have been like if chance had first thrown him among the clanless Paiute, the wealth-craving Yurok, the pedigree-mad Polynesians, or the monarchical Baganda. Proceeding from the Seneca and encountering for hundreds of miles nothing but broadly comparable social structures, Morgan prematurely generalized what primitive society was like, even though on an apparently wide inductive basis. And when he had once formulated the generalization, he could dismiss contradictory evidence from the Columbia River tribes with the cheap auxiliary hypothesis that their clan organization had fallen into decay [1936: 174].

But Morgan cannot be held responsible for the fact that so many of the tribes that he studied at first hand happened to have broadly similar social systems. He expended great effort and considerable sums of his own money to reach as many tribes as were accessible to study in the early 1860's. He could not know that northern and eastern North America would turn out to be a single major culture area in Kroeber's (1939) classification, in contrast to the much greater differentiation in western North America. Lowie's strictures with regard to premature generalization are more relevant, but in this he had much company among his contemporaries.

Leslie A. White has a more relevant evaluation of Morgan's contribution to the study of kinship:

Although Morgan failed to see that kinship in human society is primarily and essentially a social phenomenon and only secondarily and incidentally a biological matter, he did discover and appreciate the fact that relationship terms are sociological devices employed in the regulation of social life. A relationship term is a designation of an individual or class of individuals that is socially significant. Every society of human beings is divided into social classes or groups, which, with reference to any individual in the society, are designated with kinship terms. . . . One's behavior towards one's fellows varies, depending on the category of relationship in which the person stands. Since the categories are labelled with kinship terms, a close functional relationship obtains between kinship nomenclature and social organization and behavior. There are the views and postulates upon which a modern school of social anthropology bases much of its work. They were discovered, elucidated and established by Morgan many decades ago [1948: 144].

With much of White's evaluation we can readily agree. Morgan clearly recognized the social importance of kinship and was aware that the terminology formed a definite system. With regard to the functional relationships between nomenclature and behavior, Morgan recognized such relationships macroscopically but was little concerned with them at the level of the individual tribe. The Malayan system he related to particular forms of marriage, and the Ganowanian, or American Indian, system he correlated with clans. Only rarely, as in the case of the mother's brother, does he attempt to relate particular terminology to special status or behavior. Modern social anthropology is built in part on Morgan's discoveries, but most of its progress has been in the directions that Morgan neglected—the detailed structural and functional analysis of individual tribes and communities.

In modern perspective certain of Morgan's assumptions and discoveries with regard to kinship require modification. Kinship terminology is no longer considered to be the stable institution Morgan envisaged, enduring over centuries and furnishing evidence of genetic relations no longer apparent otherwise. The unity or diversity of the American Indians as a race, and their ultimate derivation from Asia, rest on evidence other than kinship terminologies. The evolutionary stages of family development are no longer tenable. Even the "classificatory" system, now that the dust of controversy has settled, has less significance than Morgan envisioned.

But, even so, it is remarkable how close to the truth he actually came. He grasped the essential principles and considered the possible explanations. That he rejected certain of the explanations that modern social anthropology accepts was in some measure due to the intellectual fashions of his time. The insights that Morgan achieved through saturation in kinship for a decade are scattered through *Systems*. And, above all, there are the raw data he collected on kinship terminologies, which become increasingly valuable as we learn more about kinship systems. In his introduction to *Systems*, Morgan says: "The tables, however, are the main result of this investigation. In their importance and value they reach far beyond any present use of their contents which this writer may be able to indicate. If they can be perfected, and the systems of the unrepresented nations be supplied, their value would be greatly increased" (1871: 8). Of his methods of comparison he was properly modest: "If these tables prove sufficient to demonstrate the utility of systems of relationship in the prosecution of ethnological investigations, one of the main objects of this work will be accomplished" (1871: 809).

In his emphasis upon *systems* of relationship and their comparison under controlled conditions, Morgan is much closer to modern scholarship than were many of his critics.

And on the basis of his pioneer insights into kinship new methods of investigation have developed that do in fact carry us far beyond the stage that Morgan had achieved. In the following chapters some of the directions that modern research has taken will be explored and the results examined.

II

THE CHOCTAW AND THEIR NEIGHBORS IN THE SOUTHEAST: ACCULTURATION UNDER PRESSURE[1]

I

WHEN I WAS A GRADUATE STUDENT IN THE EARLY 1930's, American anthropology had been going for some three decades in a direction quite opposite to that pioneered by Lewis H. Morgan. Robert H. Lowie had written *Primitive Society* (1920), in part as a critique of Morgan, and Leslie Spier had reclassified North American kinship terminologies into some eight types, while A. L. Kroeber had long advocated the view that kinship terminologies were linguistic phenomena to be analyzed in terms of psychological categories, without reference to possible sociological correlates. But when A. R. Radcliffe-Brown came to the University of Chicago in the autumn of 1931, and I became his research assistant in a proposed study of the

[1] In the preparation for this chapter I have utilized my earlier paper "Historical Changes in the Choctaw Kinship System" (1937b), as well as "Social Anthropology: Methods and Results" (1955). Swanton's numerous monographs, culminating in *Indians of the Southeastern United States* (1946), and Speck's monographs and papers provide an indispensable background, as do the historical studies of Foreman, Debo, and other historians.

Alexander Spoehr's studies (1941–47) on social and cultural change among the southeastern tribes represent one of the best controlled comparative studies yet made for American Indian tribes.

15

"Social Organization of the North American Indian," he sent me back to Morgan.

Radcliffe-Brown had been a student of W. H. R. Rivers, who had revitalized the study of social organization through a restatement of Morgan's principles as a result of his own field researches in India and Melanesia. Rivers, in *Kinship and Social Organization* (1914), concluded that "the terminology of relationship had been rigorously determined by social conditions" and especially by particular types of preferential marriage, a problem to be discussed in a later chapter. Radcliffe-Brown, on the basis of his own researches in Africa, Oceania, and Australia, had emphasized that the kinship system was composed of *both* the terminology and the patterns of social behavior between relatives and that the kinship system was an integral part of the total social structure. These conclusions had just been documented in his *Social Organization of Australian Tribes* (1931) when he put me to work assembling the available information on the kinship systems and social structures of various American Indian tribes.

One of the first series of tribes I investigated were those of the southeastern region, known generally as the "Five Civilized Tribes." Despite the fact that Morgan had personally collected some 56 out of the 80 kinship schedules he presented for the American Indian, he had made no first-hand investigations among those particular tribes. By the period 1858–62, when Morgan was planning and carrying out the first field expeditions organized to solve particular anthropological problems, the Choctaw, Creek, Chickasaw, Cherokee, and most of the Seminoles had long been removed to Indian Territory in what is now Oklahoma, and were in various stages of acculturation to white society. In addition, the tensions preceding the Civil War and the conflicts with still-wild Plains tribes made the prospects rather precarious. But the main reason he carried out no field researches was that a superior group of missionaries provided Morgan with completed schedules for all the major groups of the Southeast except the Seminole.

II

The Indians of the Southeast (see Swanton 1946) occupied a solid block of territory east of the Mississippi and conformed to a common culture type. Most of them spoke languages related to the Muskogean stock, except for the Cherokee, who were related to the Iroquoian group, and the Yuchi, who were distantly affiliated with Siouan. Their ancestors participated in the development of the Middle Mississippi archeological cultures, and they apparently expanded into the Southeast about A.D. 1400, where they were found by DeSoto in 1540. The populations were large for the area north of Mexico: the Cherokee in the Appalachian valleys of the Carolinas and Tennessee numbered about 25,000; the Creeks in Alabama, 20,000; the Seminole in Florida, about 5,000; the Choctaw in Mississippi, about 15,000; and the Chickasaw in Tennessee, about 5,000.

The population of each tribe resided in "towns" organized around a ceremonial square, with the households scattered among the fields. Subsistence was rather evenly divided between agricultural activities, which were largely in the hands of the women, and hunting, which was a male occupation. Each "town" had a civil chief and a war chief, each with assistants, and this pattern was repeated for the larger groupings into districts and tribes. Each tribe had a system of social classes as well: the chiefs and their families, honored men, warriors, and commoners— the latter not yet active in war. Because of their location between the French, Spanish, and English colonies, the Indians of the Southeast were subject to intense and vary- ing pressures in the eighteenth century which led to the formation of the Creek Confederacy, which at one time or another included most of the Indian groups in the Southeast and was, for a while, successful in resisting the advance of the colonists. But by the early nineteenth cen- tury, with the withdrawal of the French and Spanish interests in Louisiana and Florida, the pressures of Geor- gia westward across the piedmont became irresistible and led to the removal of all the tribes, except the Seminole, to Indian Territory in the 1830's.

The social structure of all the major southeastern tribes conformed to a single type, so far as it was known. Everywhere the social system was based on matrilineal descent, and the household grouping was in terms of mat- rilocal residence. Each "town" was composed of a number of matrilineal lineages and clans, usually named after ani- mals or birds—or other aspects of nature—and these lineages and clans were further grouped into larger aggre- gations called phratries or moieties. Thus the Choctaw originally had their clans grouped into two matrilineal and exogamous divisions or moieties, and their close lin- guistic relatives, The Chickasaw, had a similar dual divi- son, though it did not control marriage. The Creeks, to the east, were divided into upper and lower geographical divisions, and their matrilineal clans were organized into both a phratry and a moiety division. The Cherokee had a simpler social organization: matrilineal, exogamous clans grouped into seven pairs or phratries.

In each tribe, also, the "towns" were ordinarily grouped into districts or territorial divisions, each with a considerable degree of autonomy. The "towns," particularly among the Creeks, were further divided into "red" towns and "white" towns, the former associated with "war" and the latter with "peace," and this division was also found among some of their neighbors. Everywhere, also, there was a similar ceremonial system, centering on rituals in the town square and culminating in the harvest festival. In these rituals the social position of various groups and officials was symbolically represented, and tribal welfare and unity were expressed in ceremonial activities.

At first glance the kinship systems of the southeastern tribes also apparently conformed to a single type. In addition to the terminologies collected by various missionaries for Morgan, John R. Swanton, to whom we are indebted for most of what we know about the Indians of the southeastern United States, had independently collected genealogies and kinship terms, as well as data on certain aspects of kinship and clan behavior patterns. All the terminological systems appeared to follow a characteristic pattern known technically as the Crow type, and both Robert H. Lowie (1930) and Leslie Spier (1925) had so classified them in their various publications on kinship systems. The Crow type is well known, and both Spier and Lowie agree that its essential characteristics are the classification of the father's sister's female descendants through females with the father's sister, and their sons with the father, thus giving a definite descent pattern.

Lowie considered this classification "an overriding of the generation principle in favor of the clan or lineage principle" (1930: 105). In simpler terms, all the women of the father's matrilineal clan are classed as "aunts"—or, alternatively, as "grandmothers," and all the men as "fathers," regardless of age or generation. Correlatively, the mother's brother's children were "nephew" and "niece" (woman speaking) or "son" and "daughter" (man speaking).

But when I examined the kinship systems of the southeastern tribes (see Fig. 1) I found a whole series of variations from this typical Crow type, and the pattern of descent seemed to be somehow "turned around." In the Choctaw system, which I studied first, the father's sister's children were "father" and "father's sister," but the father's sister's son and *his* descendants through *males* were classed as "fathers," whereas the children of the father's sister's daughter became "brothers" and "sisters." Morgan is quite explicit on this point:

My father's sister's son is my father, *Ah'-ki*, whether *Ego* be a male or a female; his son is my Father again; the son of the latter is also my father; and this relationship theoretically continues downward in the male line indefinitely. The analogue of this is to be found in the infinite series of uncles among the Missouri nations: applied to the lineal male descendants of my mother's brother [1871: 191].

I had spent the previous summer on a field study of the Hopi Indians, where a Crow type of kinship system was in full operation, so I knew that this pattern of descent was something quite different from the typical Crow type.

When I looked at the data on kinship for the other southeastern tribes I found some further variations. The Chickasaw pattern of descent, as given in Morgan, is identical with that of the Crow type, except for the minor

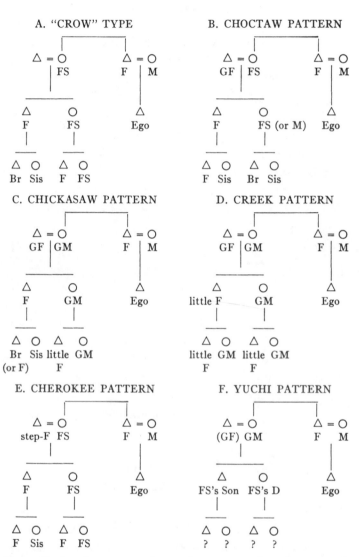

Fig. 1. Kinship Structures in the Southeast. △ is male and O is female; Ego is male in each case. The equal sign indicates marriage. English equivalents are used for the native terms: F, M, GF, GM, FS, Br, Sis, etc., standing for father, mother, grandfather, grandmother, father's sister, brother and sister, respectively. Reprinted from *American Anthropologist*, Vol. 39, No. 1, p. 37.

variation of "little father" for the father's sister's daughter's son. Swanton, however, gives "father" as an alternative to "brother" for the father's sister's son's son. The Creeks furnished another pattern of descent. Here the descendants of the father's sister, in *both* the male and the female lines, were classed as "father" and "grandmother" in both Morgan's and Swanton's accounts. The Cherokee, on the other hand, had a pattern of descent from the father's sister much like that for the Chickasaw except that the father's sister's son's son is regularly classed with the father, as are his male descendants through males. The Yuchi pattern was incomplete and will be considered separately.

III

On the basis of this preliminary survey it was possible to formulate some of the problems involved. The first problem was whether these patterns of descent represented new and fundamental types of kinship systems or were simply variations from a Crow type. As new types they would be unique, since to my knowledge they were not found anywhere else. And as *systems* they would not fit very well with what we know as to the rest of southeastern social structure. If we look at the variants, we find it possible to arrange them in a series between the Crow and Choctaw types: The Chickasaw have practically a pure Crow type, the Cherokee vary somewhat, the Creek are intermediate, and the Choctaw have almost completely reversed the line of descent. We have seen that all these tribes had a similar culture, resided in the same area, and were removed to Indian Territory under similar conditions, suggesting that the variations found might represent historical changes under the influence of common acculturative factors after removal to Oklahoma rather than being merely "random" results of unrelated circumstances.

These comparative problems were dealt with later. First, I had to find out whether there was any evidence that the Choctaw kinship system had actually changed from a Crow type. Morgan thought highly of his Choctaw schedules. The Reverends Cyrus Byington and John Edwards collaborated on one and Charles C. Copeland furnished the other; these missionaries had long resided among the Choctaw and knew their language and customs. Even so, the completion of the long and involved schedule was a difficult task, and Morgan (1871: 135) quotes Byington to the effect that "it required the united strength of the mission" to fill it out correctly. Furthermore, the two independent schedules checked remarkably well, except for minor inconsistencies; hence they must be accepted as basic data—as representing the Choctaw kinship terminology as it was in 1859. Swanton, whose data confirmed Morgan's schedules, notes (1931: 84) that his tables were "constructed in part from data collected by myself and in part from data obtained from the lists of Morgan and the entries in Byington's dictionary."

The Crow type of kinship system was recorded by Morgan in partial form among the Hidatsa and Crow of the upper Missouri and among the Pawnee, as well, but because of the earlier and more complete Choctaw schedules he was misled as to its real significance (cf. Eggan, 1960). The Crow type, in modern perspective, is an organization of kindred on the basis of the matrilineal lineage. It separates the mother's relatives from the father's relatives, but recognizes both, though in different and complementary ways. In North America we find it also among the western Pueblos, in a few tribes in aboriginal California, and in modified form on the Northwest Coast in southern Alaska and British Columbia. It also occurs in other parts of the world, notably in Melanesia and Micronesia, and is also reported for Africa and South America.

Among the Choctaw and their neighbors the aboriginal household was based on matrilocal (uxorilocal) residence and thus was composed of an extended family of three or four generations. The husband normally left his natal household to reside with his wife in a dwelling adjacent to that of his parents-in-law. Thus the women of a household represented a lineage segment related through the female line. The women were responsible for agricultural activities, and each household cultivated a neighboring plot of corn, beans, and squash in common. The men cooperated in hunting and were in historic times more and more drawn into raiding and warfare as well as into trading and other activities.

Children belonged to the clan of the mother, and the mother and her relatives were responsible for much of their education and training. A girl was under the direct control of her mother and mother's sister, while the mother's brother was responsible for the discipline of a boy and for his training in clan lore and was also important in the arrangements for marriage. The Creeks had further institutionalized certain aspects of this role in the position of the "clan uncle." The father and his relatives played a relatively minor role in these activities but were particularly important at life crises and on public ceremonial occasions. The father's natal household was a second home, where one could receive aid and comfort. The women of this household demonstrated a warm feeling for their brother's children and praised them highly at all times. The husband was initially a stranger in his wife's household and had to observe various restrictions and taboos in his relations with his wife's parents. At the same time, he played the role of mother's brother in his sister's household.

We can now see part of the reason why one's most important relatives within the household were differentiaated, since they had different tasks and responsibilities. We can also see that the father's household and lineage might be treated as a unit—all the men and women had similar roles and were classed as "fathers," and "father's sisters," respectively. These relationships were extended to closely related households, in which the women were descended from a known ancestor, and were further generalized to the clan, and even to the larger groupings under certain circumstances.

III

It should now be clear why the Choctaw kinship terminology, as recorded for Morgan, is so aberrant. For the line of males descending through males would cut right across the matrilineal lineage and clan structure, rather than coinciding with it, and the line of father's sisters would be greatly reduced. The terminological systems of the other southeastern tribes show similar cross-cutting patterns, though to lesser extents.

I concentrated my attention first on the Choctaw. On the basis of my preliminary study I came to the tentative conclusion that the Choctaw system probably represented a pure Crow type that had been altered under the stress of missionary and governmental activities and pressures. To demonstrate this working hypothesis, it would be necessary: (1) either to find the older kinship system in operation in some relatively uninfluenced region or to find an earlier account of the kinship system and then (2) to find historical evidence that would throw some light on the processes by which the changes were effected. Only then would it be profitable to extend the analysis to the other southeastern tribes and to make a detailed comparative and historical analysis.

I decided first to look for evidences of the assumed older Choctaw kinship system, and in the summer of 1933, on the advice of John R. Swanton, I visited the old Choctaw country in central Mississippi, in an attempt to find traces of older patterns among the Bogue Chito and other groups who had remained in Mississippi following the general removal of the Choctaw to Indian Territory in the 1830's. Swanton had recently published his *Source Material for the Social and Ceremonial Life of the Choctaw Indians* (1931) and had remarked on the rapid disappearance of ancient customs in Oklahoma but had added that he had obtained a considerable body of data from Mississippi informants.

This quest was completely unsuccessful, so far as my major objectives were concerned, though I gathered a considerable amount of data on the contemporary community and received a liberal education with regard to the caste system in rural Mississippi. I left Mississippi considerably discouraged and proceeded to western Oklahoma to make a preliminary study of the Cheyenne and Arapaho. In this process I drove right along the southern boundary of the Choctaw "reservation," but the Red River and its tributaries were in full flood, and I did not tarry. If I had stayed a while, I might have found the answer to my quest right there.

Later in the summer, while on the Cheyenne and Arapaho "reservation," I visited the University of Oklahoma library, and in the *Chronicles of Oklahoma* for September, 1932, I found the text of a speech that the Reverend John Edwards had made to the students of the University of California about 1880, in which he outlined the *earlier* social organization of the Choctaw. This is the same John Edwards who collaborated with the Reverend Cyrus Byington in furnishing one of the Choctaw kinship schedules for Morgan. When the Civil War broke out, he was forced to leave the Choctaw area and went to reside in California. In his lecture (edited by Swanton), entitled "The Choctaw Indians in the Middle of the Nineteenth Century" (1932: 392–425), after noting that the Choctaw "were divided into two greak *iksas,*" or moieties, within which marriage was forbidden, and that "the children all belonged to the *iksa* of the mother" and "the father was therefore a kind of interloper in his own family and had much less control of his children than his wife's brother had," he went on to make the following statements concerning the older Choctaw kinship system:

A third important principle was that kinship was not lost by remoteness. This involved a very peculiar system of nomenclature. For instance, with them, my father's brothers are all my fathers, and my mother's sisters are all my mothers, and their children are my brothers and sisters; but my mother's brother is my uncle, and his sons and daughters are mine; and my father's sister is my aunt, her son is my father, her daughter is my aunt, and *her* daughter is my aunt, and *her* daughter is my aunt, and so on, as far as it is possible to go. This is what they call *aunts* in a row. The farthest removed of one's kindred by consanguinity are aunt, uncle, nephew and niece. The line of relationship, after turning aside thus far, returns into the direct line, and becomes that of father to son, or grandfather to grandson. To us it seems a very complicated system [1932; 400–401].

Here was clear, unequivocal, documentary proof that the Choctaw formerly had a pure Crow type of kinship system. Needless to say, I was slightly annoyed at Swanton for not having mentioned Edward's account, but he may have thought that a summer in Mississippi would be good for me.

There was firm evidence, then, for a definite change in the Choctaw kinship system from the time of removal in the 1830's to the time when Morgan received the schedules in 1859. I could now turn to the second part of my problem: Can the influences affecting the Choctaw from the time of removal to the Civil War be historically controlled? Fortunately, this question could soon be answered in the affirmative. During the following year Grant Foreman, a distinguished historian, published his study of *The Five Civilized Tribes* (1934), of which Book I was devoted to the Choctaw; and Angie Debo surveyed a somewhat longer period in *The Rise and Fall of the Choctaw Republic* (1934).

Briefly, the Choctaw were subjected to longer and more intensive acculturational influences than were the Chickasaw, Creek, or Cherokee. Even before removal the Choctaw were aiding the United States against the Creeks and the British, and missions were established among them as early as 1818, and schools soon after. They were the first tribe from the Southeast to move to Indian Territory after the Treaty of Dancing Rabbit Creek, though the tribe was bitterly divided and more than a third of the Choctaw Nation refused to remove initially. But in the thirty years 1830–60 they had set up a new system of government on the model of our territorial governments; developed a comprehensive law code, which was a mixture of English law and Choctaw custom; modernized marriage practices through abolishing clan exogamy; and modified the laws regarding property and inheritance.

There are numerous statements in Foreman indicating the efforts—and successes—of missionaries, teachers, and government agents in changing the attitudes and mode of life of the Choctaw. The facts that women worked in the fields and that a father—in accordance with the matrilineal system of inheritance—failed to provide for his own children particularly worried the missionaries. New regulations regarding land were introduced that emphasized the position of the man as head of the family. Marriage was regulated by law, widows were entitled to dower rights, and children could inherit their father's estate. The leaders no longer came from the clans but were elected by the adult male members of the district, and the old town rituals were largely replaced by the church and its activities.

The effect of these changes on the social organization of the Choctaw was to break down the clan and kinship structures and to emphasize the nuclear family and the territorial tie. In the later periods the clan structure became largely a memory, many Choctaw not even knowing their own clans. In general terms, these changes indicate a shift from a matrilineal to a patrilineal, or bilateral, emphasis, though the agents of acculturation were not always aware of the significance of the changes they were bringing about. Specifically, these changes seem to have affected the kinship structure first by "turning around" the pattern of descent from the father's sister, making "fathers" descend in the male line, rather than "father's sisters" in the female line, as Edwards reports for the old Choctaw system.

This tentative conclusion, if it is to have any *general* value, should also "explain" the changes that have taken place in the other tribes of the Southeast who were also removed and subjected to parallel influences. Foreman presents evidence to indicate that the Chickasaw and Creek were considerably behind the Choctaw in general "progress" up to the Civil War. The Chickasaw, in particular, were backward. They had been less sedentary and more warlike in the Southeast, and their removal to Indian Territory took place later and under less favorable circumstances. They were settled on the western portion of the Choctaw reservation, where they were continually harassed by the unpacified Plains tribes. They refused to merge with the Choctaw, and missions and schools did not get under way in their territory until after 1847. Hence the Chickasaw retained their aboriginal customs to a much greater degree and for a longer period of time than did the Choctaw. The Creek, on the other hand, made more rapid "progress" than the Chickasaw. Initially, they were suspicious of the efforts of missionaries to change their customs and expelled them from the Creek Nation in 1836, but the missionaries were allowed to return in 1842, and their influence gradually increased. During the decade of the 1840's a few schools were established and chiefs were beginning to be elected, and by the 1850's many changes were in progress: new laws were replacing old customs, property was being inherited according to new legal provisions, schools were well established, men were doing the agricultural work, and missions were expanding.

On the basis of Grant Foreman's account it is possible

to arrange the Choctaw, Chickasaw, and Creek in a rough series, insofar as the *general degree* of acculturation is concerned. In the period up to the Civil War, the Choctaw were subjected to the greatest influence, the Chickasaw the least, and the Creek were in between. The Chickasaw had a Crow-type kinship system in Morgan's time and the Choctaw had had one two generations earlier. There is some documentary evidence to indicate that the Creek also formerly had a Crow type of kinship structure. Swanton quotes from the George Stiggins manuscript of the early nineteenth centry, which states: "All the men of the father's clan or family are called father, the women are generally called their grandmother, all the men of the mother's family older than themselves are their uncles, being their mother's brothers" (1928: 87). But Swanton, in his own studies of Creek social organization, had recorded the same pattern of kinship terminology as is found in Morgan and hence noted that the kinship terms used may cut across clan lines rather than coinciding with them. In the context that we have suggested it seems clear that both Stiggins and Swanton were right and that the Creeks had modified the application of terms for the descendants of the father's sister in the directions stated above. Hence we have a series of variations in kinship terminology for these three tribes corresponding rather precisely with the general degree of acculturation that they have experienced and to which they have responded.

The Cherokee furnish an additional and independent group against which to test our preliminary conclusions. They belong to a different linguistic stock and have a somewhat different early history. On the other hand, they were removed to Indian Territory and subjected to much the same acculturational influences that affected the other tribes, though, if we may judge by Foreman's account, these pressures were less intensive for them in the period before the Civil War than they were for the Choctaw. There were difficulties with removal, though one group had voluntarily moved to Arkansas at an earlier period, and the "eastern" Cherokee were forcibly removed in 1838, but many managed to escape. Again, white influences brought about a change in the position of women, and there were new divisions of labor, new laws and governmental processes, and a national school system, though they did not become well established until the 1850's.

The small group of Cherokee who remained in the hills of North Carolina were studied by W. H. Gilbert, Jr., a fellow graduate student, in the early 1930's, and he found exactly the situation that I had hoped to find among the Mississippi Choctaw. Among the older people on the eastern Cherokee Reservation he found (1937) a Crow-type kinship system still in operation, though complicated in part by patterns of preferential marriage. In Oklahoma, on the other hand, the Cherokee had changed a step beyond the Creek pattern at the time of the Civil War.

Acculturational influences in North Carolina were less intensive but were operating in the same direction. Thus Gilbert mentions (n.d.: 278) the loss of political power of clan heads, the decline in family control, particularly with regard to marriage, the loss of authority on the part of the mother's brother, and the adoption of family names on the American pattern, which "has tended to shift the emphasis in lineality to the paternal ancestry." This shift in emphasis from the matrilineal to the patrilineal line among the eastern Cherokee should result in similar changes in the patterns of descent, assuming that other factors remain the same.

IV

The Yuchi, Natchez, and other groups in the Southeast represent a more complicated problem, in part because the available data are more fragmentary and in part because these tribes developed certain specializations on the common basic social institutions that we have noted for the Southeast. The Yuchi were studied by Speck in 1904–5 when they resided in Oklahoma in three scattered settlements in the northwestern corner of the Creek Nation. The Yuchi spoke a separate language, distantly related to Siouan, and had belonged to the Creek Confederation, being removed to Indian Territory with the Creeks. But in Speck's time the remnant population mixed little with the Creeks and were friendly with the Shawnee and the Sauk and Fox.

The Yuchi were divided into matrilineal exogamous clans named after animals, but these clans were cross-cut by a division of the men into two patrilineal societies called "chiefs" and "warriors," which were symbolically associated with peace and war, respectively, and which were important in the ceremonial, military, and political life. These dual organizations tended toward endogamy in that a "chief" preferred his daughters to marry other "chiefs," but they never developed into a full-fledged double descent system—a step that would have made the Yuchi unique in North America.

The aboriginal Yuchi kinship system is incompletely

known, but Speck (1909) recorded the father's sister as classed with the grandmother, and the father's sister's husband as "grandfather," while the father's sister's children were called by descriptive terms. It seems probable that by Speck's time the Yuchi kinship system was already considerably modified. The classification of the father's sister is suggestive of a Crow type of system, especially when coupled with matrilineal clans, but the use of descriptive terms for her descendants suggests a breakdown of the system.

More recently, Dr. Günter Wagner, in the course of a linguistic study of the Yuchi, recorded a list of the current (1933) terms, which he was kind enough to send me. These give an "Omaha" type of structure: the father's sister is now called "little mother," and her children are "nephew" and "niece" (male speaking) or "little son" and "little daughter" (female speaking). The father's sister's husband is still classed with the grandfather, however. The children of the mother's brother are correspondingly "mother's brother" and "little mother."

There is thus considerable evidence that the Yuchi have gone through the whole sequence of changes from a Crow to an Omaha type of kinship system. One possible factor is the greater emphasis on patrilineal institutions among the Yuchi, as evidenced by the "peace" and "war" societies. But for the later stages of this change the evidence of close contacts with the Shawnee and the Sauk and Fox, both of which have an Omaha type of system, is undoubtedly significant.

Speck, in a brief note (1939: 171–72) has added further information on this interesting situation by indicating that there was considerable intermarriage with both Shawnee and Creek. He agrees substantially with the analysis given above and regards the Yuchi as an "example of deviation from a former and more solid social pattern subsequent to their dispersion from Georgia and their incorporation among the Creek towns." He goes on to point out that the Catawba, a Siouan group in the Southeast, are also far advanced in acculturation but that their kinship system reflects interaction with the Carolina Whites.

For other groups in the Southeast, including the Natchez and Chitimacha near the Mississippi River and the Calusa in Florida, we have evidence of specialized systems of social stratification and complex marriage patterns, but little in the way of data on kinship. Mary Haas has assembled all the data we are likely to get on "Natchez and Chitimacha Clans and Kinship Terminology" (1939), and her linguistic researches enable her to correct and amplify Swanton's fragmentary data for the Natchez. She adduces comparative evidence to suggest that the matrilineal clan system may be a recent adoption from the Creeks, among whom the surviving Natchez resided in Georgia, after the breakdown of their class system. With regard to kinship terms she finds a special term for father's sister, which is used also for her daughter and daughter's daughter, while the father's sister's son and the father's sister's husband are both called "little father's brother." She notes (1939: 609) that the system is contradictory in several respects, which she thinks is due "to the fact that the Natchez system has been greatly influenced by the Creek system." The Chitimacha, who had some kind of caste system, apparently did not possess a clan system, and the kinship system is fragmentary and confused: "it has probably been broken down due to long contact with the Louisiana French," according to Haas (1939: 610).

The Natchez class system, as reported by French observers, was composed of an upper class divided into Suns, Nobles, and Honored people and a lower class of Stinkards or commoners. Descent in this system was matrilineal, and the two classes were exogamous, with a special provision that the descendants of males in the upper classes dropped a step downward. J. L. Fischer has recently reviewed the "Solutions to the Natchez Paradox" (1964)—since the system as described could not operate for very long—and has added one of his own.

For the Calusa of southern Florida, Goggin and Sturtevant (1964) have brought together the archeological and ethno-historical data, which indicate that this fairly large but non-agricultural group had a complex stratified society with elaborate religious activities and considerable technological development. According to these authors:

The Calusa, in a highly favorable environment, developed South Florida culture to a real climax—they shared many social, political, and technological traits with their neighbors, but were able to elaborate these patterns to such a degree that Calusa culture as a whole takes on quite a different cast [1964: 208].

But the Calusa, unlike the Natchez, do not seem to be a specialization on a Southeast-type sociocultural base.

v

The immediate conclusions that may be drawn from this brief survey of the Choctaw and their neighbors in the Southeast can be briefly summarized.

(1) The evidence indicates that a Crow type of kinship structure was widespread in the Southeast. The

Choctaw, Chickasaw, Creek, and Cherokee all had such a system in early times.

(2) These kinship structures, originally Crow in type, were progressively modified by being subjected to varying degrees of the same acculturational processes. For the Choctaw, Chickasaw, and Creek there is a close correlation between the degree of acculturation and the degree of modification of the kinship pattern. The independent evidence available for the Cherokee confirms this correlation, as does the more fragmentary data for the Yuchi.

These conclusions have a firm foundation in documentary and comparative evidence, and they make it possible to reconcile apparent inconsistencies between accounts for different periods in a productive manner. But they also raise a whole series of new problems that have important implications for kinship theory and for studies of social and cultural change.

If we turn first to Lewis H. Morgan's own contributions to kinship theory, we see that some of them have stood the test of time and others are in need of modification. Morgan's conception of kinship terminology as a *system,* and his belief that the kinship system is related to other aspects of social structure, are still central to our thinking. Without the concept of a *system,* the Choctaw, Chickasaw, Creek, and Cherokee variants have no meaning beyond being linguistic phenomena or historical "accidents." Morgan conceived of kinship terminologies as reflecting social conditions, such as clans and forms of marriage, but he thought in macroscopic terms and great stages—the America Indian system was essentially one and was based on the clan system. But Morgan's model for this "classificatory" kinship system was that of the Iroquois Indians: a bilaterally organized system without much reference to the matrilineal clan system, which they also possessed. Hence Morgan was not sensitized to the possibility that kinship terminologies might reflect clan organization in much more direct fashion. And we have seen that the Choctaw system, on which he put such heavy reliance, was already profoundly modified from the Crow type of lineage system. Hence, when he later discovered the Crow type among the Pawnee, Hidatsa, and Crow Indians, he treated it as a "variant" of the Choctaw type, rather than vice versa, and thus was prevented from seeing its true significance.

The evidence we have presented from the Southeast also denies Morgan's major assumption that kinship terminologies are basic and unchanging over long periods of time and hence can be utilized to discover historical relationships between peoples long separated. In the Southeast, patterns of kinship terminology have turned out to be remarkably sensitive indicators of social and cultural change—and over periods of a few generations, or even less. Morgan was correct in assuming that *patterns* of kinship terminology were almost never borrowed, though individual terms might be replaced, but he thought of these patterns as comparable to the unconscious patterns of linguistic structure and assumed that they were transmitted "with the blood." As such they were not amenable to the kinds of influences that we have shown were in fact operative.

A further difficulty is in no way a criticism of Morgan: that is, that the kinship systems he so carefully assembled a century ago do not, in all cases, represent the aboriginal systems unmodified by white acculturation. Once we make this discovery, a whole new set of problems arises. When the *League of the Iroquois* was published in 1851, that nation had undergone over three hundred years of contact and acculturation, and we know from comparative study of the Iroquois tribes and from Father Lafitau's observations in the early eighteenth century that their kinship systems had already undergone certain changes.

With regard to the specific changes in the southeastern kinship systems it is clear that the traditional Americanist explanation in terms of borrowing does not help very much. Here there have been few lexical changes; rather, the terms have changed primarily with regard to their application and hence their meaning. These changes in pattern seem progressive and not easily subject to borrowing, especially when they pertain to distant relatives.

The historical data on the Southeast do not tell us precisely what the process of change was, but what acculturation apparently did was to modify the attitudes and behavior patterns toward various relatives. Thus the relationships of a father to his child were strengthened at the expense of the mother's brother. The father came to own land and property and to be head of an elementary family. In this process the clan was weakened, losing its corporate functions and political power, and matrilineal descent was no longer of much significance. It is this change in behavior patterns that seems to be the medium through which kinship terminological patterns were modified, and it is consonant with the modern view, stemming from Rivers, Lowie, and Radcliffe-Brown, that there is normally a close correlation between the terminological structure and the social behavior of relatives.

This initial study of the Southeast also convinced me that it was possible to combine "functional" and "historical" points of view without doing violence to either. In studies of acculturation both would seem to be essential—

we need to know something of the interrelations of social institutions before we can deal adequately with social and cultural change. And as Alex Spoehr has pointed out: "The very meaning of functional dependence is that change in one variable results in change in a dependent variable" (1950: 11). Without the concept of a *kinship system,* the changes recorded in terminology for the southeastern tribes have very little meaning, and without the *historical analysis,* the kinship structure remains blurred. Here one document turned out to be more significant than several months of field research. Comparative evidence is important, but as Boas long ago noted, the results can be read both ways. With the added *historical* controls, however, the directions of change are clear and the comparisons may be utilized to give a more detailed picture of the steps in social and cultural change. Here their internal consistency is additional evidence that we are on the right track.

The general conclusions have a wider application. They may serve as a working hypothesis for the consideration of other social systems undergoing acculturative influences, and we shall see some examples in later chapters. In terms of an ultimate interest in systematic general "laws," we have here an instance supporting Radcliffe-Brown's hypothesis that "any marked inconsistency in a social system tends to induce change" (1935: 533–34). The kinship systems of the southeastern tribes have partially recovered their internal consistency by means of a series of similar changes.

That was as far as I had gotten with these problems when I had an opportunity to go to the Philippines for a year, and on my return I was too busy with other projects to pursue them further. But one of the satisfactions of teaching is to have a student who gets interested in a set of problems and carries them much further than you have done.

A few years later, Alexander Spoehr, then a graduate student at the University of Chicago, decided to test some of these hypotheses against additional data, both from the field and from documentary sources. He turned his attention first to the Seminole, an early offshoot of the Creeks in the eighteenth century, who had fled to Spanish Florida and had stubbornly resisted removal to Oklahoma until after a long and costly war with the newly established United States. In addition, Spoehr made a survey of Creek, Cherokee, and Choctaw communities in Oklahoma, where he found a wide range of variant kinship patterns still in operation.

The Florida Seminole in 1939 were a small but highly conservative group, still technically "at war" with the United States, and Spoehr (1941) found a matrilineal clan system and a Crow type of kinship system in full operation, along with an extended family organization based on matrilocal residence. The reduction in population and number of clans had affected marriage regulations, leading to considerable marriage into the father's clan. But the behavior patterns reported for the Creeks and their neighbors in the earlier literature were here in

actual operation, with changes as a result of white acculturation just beginning to take effect.

The Seminole were not finally removed to Oklahoma
until 1843 and were ultimately settled just west of the
Creek reservation, where they were relatively isolated and
were able to retain many of their customs until 1903,
when their lands were allotted, after which they changed
much more rapidly. Spoehr (1942) found that the old
"town" organization and much of the clan system remained important up to 1900 and that the kinship system
conformed to the basic Crow type in all essentials, with
behavior patterns corresponding to those reported for
the earlier Creeks. After 1900 the changes he found paral-
leled those noted for the other southeastern tribes, though
they had not proceeded as far.

The Seminole thus provide additional evidence con-
firming the hypothesis of a basic Crow type of kinship
system in the Southeast, which changed under white
pressures in the direction of the new values. And, since
the Seminole are a direct offshoot of the Creek and were
less acculturated, they provide further evidence that the
Creek also had a Crow type of kinship organization and
confirm the brief statements in the Stiggins manuscript,
written in 1831 (Swanton 1928: 87).

But Spoehr was able to go considerably further. In
his 1938–39 field surveys (Spoehr 1947) of contemporary
Creek, Cherokee, and Choctaw social systems in Oklahoma, he was able to find all the variants we have noted
still in operation—and additional ones besides. By cor-
relating them with the degree of conservatism or progress
in different regions, he was able to outline the sequence
of changes in each tribe in considerable detail. Among
the Creeks, for example, he was able to work out the

whole sequence of changes from a pure Crow type, based on the matrilineal lineage, to a straight "generation" pattern, with all cousins classed as "brothers" and "sisters." The Oklahoma Cherokee, more advanced, had shifted to a "generation" pattern, with few traces of the earlier system, which still survived among the eastern Cherokee in the Smoky Mountains. And among the Choctaw, Spoehr found several isolated communities where a straight Crow type of kinship system was still in operation, though others showed various stages of change. (You can imagine my own embarrassment, since I had driven through this very region, en route from the Mississippi Choctaw to western Oklahoma, without stopping to investigate.)

Spoehr was also able to correlate this regular series of changes much more definitely with the changes in related aspects of social organization: the reduction in the size of the family group and its shift from a "consanguine" to a "conjugal" form, to use Linton's terminology; the loss of such clan functions as the control of marriage and extension of kinship, the punishment of murder and other wrongs, and the control of education and etiquette; and the breakup of the old "town" organization and its replacement with a church-centered community. Not all these changes proceeded together but they were interrelated in complex ways. Spoehr found that the changes in the application of kinship terms tended to lag behind other social changes, thus reflecting them rather than leading the way.

The stimulus to change Spoehr finds in the contact situation, and he notes that the principal contact agents in the nineteenth century were the white settler, the missionary, and the government agent—the latter including the military—and he briefly analyzes their activities up to the time of allotment of the reservations. The series of changes he had outlined he finds reflected in terms of the contact situation—similar changes resulted from similar acculturational pressures, and the rates of change reflect differing degrees of intensity of the contacts. And, as is the case with all good studies, he has provided us with a series of new problems for further investigation.

III

THE CHEYENNE AND ARAPAHO IN THE PERSPECTIVE OF THE PLAINS: ECOLOGY AND SOCIETY[1]

I

IN THE LAST CHAPTER WE EXAMINED SOME OF LEWIS H. Morgan's conceptions of social organization against the data that has since become available on the Indians of the Southeast. In particular we examined the variations in social structure against the historical background of acculturation to white pressures during the nineteenth-century and came to the conclusion that there was a close correlation between the degree of acculturation and the degree of modification of the kinship and clan patterns. In this process we saw the importance of Morgan's concept of a *kinship system,* as well as the reasons why he did not recognize the close relations that in fact exist between the matrilineal clan or lineage and the "Crow" type of kinship system. But we also saw that kinship terminology, far from being an immutable system transmit-

[1] I have drawn on a number of my earlier studies in the preparation of this chapter, notably "The Cheyenne and Arapaho Kinship Systems" (1937), "The Ethnological Cultures and Their Archeological Backgrounds" (1952), and "Social Anthropology: Methods and Results" (1955). I am also indebted to the classic studies of Wissler, Lowie, and Spier on the Plains and to Julian Steward's *Theory of Cultural Change* (1955) and Waldo Wedel's articles and monographs on Plains archeology and environment.

45

ted "with the blood" from distant common ancestors, is closely related to the patterns of social behavior between relatives and is a sensitive indicator of social and cultural change.

I wish now to turn our attention to a consideration of the Indian tribes of a neighboring region, the Great Plains, and examine Morgan's contributions to our understanding of Plains social organization in the light of my own and others' researches. Here we shall see that ecological factors are related to the forms of society that we find in the Plains, and we shall need to examine the relative efficiency of different adaptations to the environment. Here we shall also be concerned with social and cultural change, but in terms of the achievement of a common pattern of social structure in the High Plains.

In contrast to the situation in the Southeast, Morgan personally collected for the Plains area the bulk of the data on kinship and social organization that he presented in *Systems of Consanguinity and Affinity of the Human Family* (1871). During his field trips to the Missouri River region in the summers of 1859–62, he secured kinship schedules and other data for some nineteen tribes, mostly from the eastern or Prairie Plains but with a fair representation from the northern High Plains. There, half a century after Lewis and Clark, Morgan visited the newly established reservations and mission stations in Kansas and Nebraska Territory and the upper Missouri region, all the way to the army posts at the foot of the Rockies. The mode of travel on the Missouri River a century ago was by shallow-draft steamships, which supplied the trading posts and government forts, and Morgan's *Indian Journals, 1859–62,* give a fascinating account of the frontier at that period. River travel and the unsettled condi-

tions beyond the frontier made it impossible for Morgan
to secure adequate data on the tribes of the central and
southern High Plains, but he was able to collect considerable information on certain of these groups from traders
and fellow passengers.

The greatest problem that Morgan faced in his research, once he was in the field, was one of communication. With the Iroquois in New York he had found willing
and intelligent interpreters who were at home in English.
On the frontier the potentially most useful informants
were ignorant of English, and adequate interpreters were
few and far between. Morgan found Indian women to be
the best source for kinship data, and he utilized as informants and translators a varied group of missionaries, traders,
half-breeds, and men who had grown up among Indians.
It was his experience that very few whites had acquired
the linguistic competence to fill out his schedules unaided.

Almost half of all the kinship schedules that Morgan
personally collected and published in *Systems* were from
the Plains area. He organized his data in terms of the
major language families, which were surprisingly well
known for that period. Thus for tribes of the Siouan stock,
he presents kinship data for the Dakota proper and their
subdivisions, the Sisseton, Yankton, and Teton, as well as
the Assiniboin, an earlier offshoot; the Omaha, Ponca, and
Kansa, who (with the Osage and Quapaw) make up the
Dhegiha division; the Iowa and Oto, who, along with
the Winnebago, make up the Chiwere division; and the
Mandan, Hidatsa, and related Crow, who resided on the
upper Missouri. For the Algonkian stock he recorded data
on the various Cree divisions (including the Plains Cree),
the Potawatomi, the Cheyenne, Gros Ventre, Blackfoot,
and Blood, as well as various Central Algonkian tribes

recently removed to Kansas reservations. In addition, he secured some data on the Pawnee and Arikara, Caddoan-speaking groups on the Prairie Plains.

In his analysis and discussion of these kinship systems Morgan discovered further evidence that all of them conformed to his "classificatory" type based on the Iroquois model. He was concerned with the apparent lack of clans among the Dakota tribes but was more impressed with the enduring nature of the kinship system: "We shall be led step-by-step to the final inference that this system originated in the primitive ages of mankind, and that it had been propagated like language with the streams of the blood" (1871: 176). With his eyes fixed on this ultimate goal, he neglected some important variations in the data immediately before him.

Thus the Central Siouans of the Missouri River region, who were organized in patrilineal clans and formed a compact cultural grouping, were related linguistically to the apparently clanless Dakota and agreed with them in the "ten indicative features" of the "classificatory" kinship system, but they also presented some striking differences, particularly with regard to the classification of cross-cousins. Thus, the mother's brother's children, instead of being called "cousin" were called "mother's brother" and "mother," and this pattern descended in the male line indefinitely; correlatively, the children of the father's sister were "nephew" and "niece" (male speaking) or "son" and "daughter" (female speaking). Morgan carefully checked this strange terminology on a number of reservations and found it uniform. If he had not been so wedded to the Iroquois system as the model for a clan-organized society, he might have noted the correlation of the "line of uncles" with the mother's patrilineage and clan **and** thus defined the modern "Omaha" pattern of kinship. For, as Lowie (1917b: 152–54) long ago pointed out, these Central Siouan systems provide much better evidence of clan orientation than do the Iroquois and Dakota.[2]

Morgan's data for the village tribes of the upper Missouri, particularly the Mandan and Hidatsa, with the related Crow of Montana, were incomplete, but he did establish the fact that they had matrilineal clans and that the Hidatsa and Crow classified the children of the father's sister as "father" and "mother." In the last chapter we noted the reasons by which Morgan was prevented from realizing the true nature of the Choctaw kinship pattern; when he later found the "Crow" pattern of descent from the father's sister among the Pawnee, he considered it a "variant" of the Choctaw form rather than the basic type. This "Crow" type is correlated with matrilineal descent and is thus structurally equivalent to the "Omaha" system, though with a reversed descent pattern.

There were, then, in Morgan's data for the Plains region, at least three variant patterns of kinship grouping within his broadly defined "classificatory" system. We shall soon see that there was still a fourth variant, which was dominant on the High Plains but for which Morgan had no clear evidence. Here we shall be primarily concerned with the further definition and classification of these types, their relation to environmental or ecological conditions, and their correlation with other aspects of

[2] Floyd Lounsbury (1964) has recently challenged the existence of this relationship in a number of cases, but I think the examples he uses can be shown to be the results of recent changes under acculturative influences. Charles Callender's recent monograph, *The Social Organization of the Central Algonkians* (1962), is relevant in this connection.

society and culture. We shall then be able to assess more adequately the changes that were taking place in the High Plains during the historical period.

II

When I first went to study the Cheyenne and Arapaho in Oklahoma in the summer of 1933, the Plains was our best known culture area and its inhabitants had come to be the most "typical" of all our Indians. The American Museum of Natural History, under the direction of Clark Wissler, had sponsored an elaborate series of comparative studies of the Sun Dance, Plains age-societies, material culture, and ceremonies, and there were monographs by professional anthropologists on almost every major tribe. But, with regard to kinship, our knowledge of the Plains tribes was little advanced over that of Morgan's time—for reasons that we have briefly noted. Thus, when Leslie Spier classified the kinship systems of North America, in 1925, into some eight empirical types, based largely on the terminology for cross-cousins, the various Plains tribes were distributed in six of them, but several prominent groups in the central and southern plains were not represented at all.

Hence I concentrated my attention first on the social systems of the Cheyenne and Arapaho, who by then had come to be considered among the most typical of the High Plains tribes and, utilizing the Cheyenne kinship system as a "model," attempted a preliminary interpretation of kinship in the Plains area. During the 1930's a number of studies were made among neighboring groups: the Kiowa, Kiowa-Apache, Comanche, Mescalero, Lipan, and Teton Dakota, which provided comparative data and enabled me to make a more satisfactory classification of Plains kinship systems into two major types (1937: 89–93) —(1) a "generational" type and (2) a "lineage" type— and to account for the variants in terms of adaptation to the ecological and social conditions of Plains life.

The Indian tribes who occupied the High Plains and prairie margins were semi-nomadic warriors and hunters of bison or buffalo. The plains were the main habitat of the American bison and the most typical Plains tribes depended on the bison almost entirely for food, clothing, and shelter. West of the plains, in the deserts of the Great Basin, the Shoshonean-speaking nomadic food-gatherers lived on the margins of subsistence. The eastern tribes in the Prairie Plains, on the other hand, combined agriculture with hunting and lived in sedentary villages for most of the year, traveling to the High Plains to hunt buffalo during the summer.

The first accounts of Plains life come from the Coronado expedition of 1540–42, which, traveling eastward from the Rio Grande into what is now Texas, reported Indians living like Arabs and following the herds of "cows," using dogs to transport their tents on travois frames. Two centuries later, a much more elaborate and intensified pattern of life was discovered in the northern plains, centered on the utilization of the horse, which had spread from the New Mexico Spanish settlements after A.D. 1600, and which lasted until the extinction of the buffalo herds in the 1880's and the subsequent reservation period.

Wissler, in his well-known culture-area classification (1917, 1922), presented a broad view of the plains, including not only the central High Plains but the Prairie

Plains on the east and north and much of the Great Basin as well. Within this broad area, he singled out as the "typical" Plains tribes some eleven groups who occupied the central High Plains and considered the rest as "marginal" to this culture center, exhibiting the trait complexes of the typical tribes in lesser intensities and varying degrees. Wissler thought of the horse as intensifying and enriching the earlier Plains culture pattern, but not seriously modifying it. Plains culture was essentially "timeless," and, while Wissler was aware of ecological factors as somehow related to the development of the culture center, he did not carry their analysis far enough.

A. L. Kroeber (1939), in a notable revision of the culture-area classification two decades later, made a clearer separation of the High, or short-grass, Plains and the Prairie Plains, though he included both within a single enlarged "Eastern and Northern Culture Area," which encompassed most of the region east of the Rocky Mountains. Kroeber, considering culture wholes rather than trait complexes, also took issue with Wissler's view of Plains culture, arguing that the plains had been only marginally and sparsely occupied before the horse and that the introduction of the horse had revolutionized the possibilities of Plains life and had led marginal peoples to abandon their settled agricultural life and develop new cultural patterns and values. This apparent shift was further supported by W. D. Strong's (1935, 1940) archeological researches in Nebraska, which showed evidence of earlier sedentary occupations and traced such groups as the Cheyenne back to their abandoned earth-lodge villages east of the Missouri River.

Since then there have been numerous specialized studies on various aspects of Plains life, and S. C. Oliver has recently published an important essay, *Ecology and Cultural Continuity as Contributing Factors in the Social Organization of the Plains Indians* (1962), which both supports and extends my own point of view as to the nature of Plains social structure and the factors affecting it.

III

All the typical tribes of the High Plains were divided into a number of bands, which camped and hunted independently for much of the year. These bands varied in size but were relatively large and often centered on a core of siblings and close relatives of the leader or chief, but anyone was free to join, whether related or not. The typical band might range in size from 150 to 500 persons but would increase or decrease according to the fortunes of warfare and hunting—hence leadership counted for a good deal.

The tribal organization came into operation during the summer months, when the bands of each tribe assembled at some selected spot in a great camp circle. Each band had its position in the circle, and for many groups the circle symbolized a great lodge embracing the whole tribe. With the formation of the camp circle a whole series of dormant institutions came to life: a political organization composed of selected chiefs set up a lodge in the center, a series of military or warrior societies emerged into action, and ritual activities centering on sacred bundles had a prominent position. Each summer one of the war societies was selected as the camp police, acting as the enforcement agency for the council of chiefs. Their main task was to organize and police the communal hunts, where disobedience of the rules might endanger the food supply of the whole community. On these occasions they had the power to whip offenders and destroy their property.

This oscillation between the band and the camp circle was closely related to the habits of the buffalo, on whom the High Plains tribes primarily depended. During the fall and winter the buffalo herds broke up into small groups and scattered widely, seeking shelter and forage. The various tribes did likewise, not from cultural habit but from necessity. The Cheyenne say they once tried to stay together as a tribe in the early nineteenth century and almost starved to death—they never tried it again. In the late spring and early summer, as grass became available, the buffalo began to congregate in larger and larger numbers for the mating season. The tribal bands also began to assemble, both for communal hunting and for the performance of tribal and social rituals. A few groups, the Comanche in the southern plains and the Crow and Dakota in the north, were aberrant in certain respects, for reasons that will be touched on later.

The development of collective hunting methods was essential to the survival of large groups on the plains. Driving game into a pound is an ancient practice among northern hunting peoples in both Asia and North America, and on the northern plains buffalo were driven in converging lines into a corral, or over a cliff, even in prehorse days. The "surround," in which buffalo were encircled and forced to "mill" around, was used on the southern plains before the acquisition of the horse but became much more efficient with the horse, since larger numbers could be killed in this manner on the open plains. This greater efficiency of group hunting, as over against individual enterprise, was reflected both in the tribal organization during the summer and in the sanctions that were enforced at that time.

The patterns of warfare and raiding in the plains affected both size and prestige. Tribes had to maintain hunting areas in order to survive, and smaller groups often established symbiotic relations with larger tribes, as when the Kiowa-Apache became a band in the Kiowa camp circle and when the Sarsi joined the Blackfoot confederacy. Horses were normally secured by trade or by raiding and theft, and status was acquired by such means, as well as in combat. Only the Comanche became involved in horse-raising or normally used horses for food. There was apparently also an upper limit on the number of people who could assemble in the camp circle, which may be one reason why the Dakota groups and the Comanche divided into subtribes as population increased.

The unity of the tribe was represented in a set of sacred symbols and in the performance of tribal rituals. The Cheyenne, for example, had four sacred medicine arrows, which were symbolically associated with the welfare of the tribe. A murder within the tribe polluted the arrows, which then had to be cleansed and renewed by their keeper in a special ceremony. The Sun Dance was performed by all the High Plains groups in much the same way, though the organization for carrying it out varied considerably. The Cheyenne performed it as a result of an individual vow, but the whole tribal organization was involved in one way or another, and the rituals pertained both to the fertility of the tribe and to the buffalo, on which so much depended.

Within the tribe and band, kinship was both important and widely extended. The kinship terminology was bilateral and conformed to the "classificatory" pattern that Morgan had established. But the specific Iroquois pattern of cousin terminology was restricted to the Dakota tribes and the Plains Cree and Ojibwa in the prairie margins. The Cheyenne and Arapaho, and the great bulk of the High Plains tribes, were organized primarily in terms of generations, and all one's cousins, both parallel and cross-, were classed as "brothers" and "sisters," as far as they could be traced on both sides. Relatives had important responsibilities for aid and support, and there was a close correlation between the patterns of social behavior between relatives and the terminological groupings.

Marriage was not regulated by clan exogamy, except for the Crow, but was outside the known range of relationships and thus served to integrate kinship groups within the band and tribe. Marriages were generally arranged by the families concerned, though the young men preferred to "elope" first, if possible, and there were important and continuing exchanges of horses, lodges, clothing, and food between the two sets of relatives. Residence was variable but almost always with relatives, thus creating an enlarged or extended household group. Among the Cheyenne and Arapaho the couple normally resided in a lodge adjacent to the wife's parents, forming an extended family "camp," which was the basic economic unit of the band and within which an elaborate set of "respect" and "joking" behaviors aided in ameliorating the tensions and conflicts of interest. Among the Kiowa the nucleus of the "camp" was a group of siblings and their spouses, the Blackfoot groups apparently favored patrilocal or virilocal residence, and the Dakota preferred a bilateral extended family group where possible. The independent nuclear family was apparently too small a unit for hunting and protection, even during the fall and winter, and seldom was found alone.

Morgan's data for these High Plains groups were fragmentary and incomplete. Thus his data for the Cheyenne came from a French trader who had lived among them for many years and was fluent in the language. However, he could not remember the terms used for cross-cousins, and Morgan suggested that they might follow the "Omaha" pattern, as we have defined it. His best data on kinship was for the Crow, which he secured with the assistance of Robert Meldrum, a trader with the American Fur Company, who had lived among the Crow and was married to a Crow woman. The Crow were organized in terms of matrilineal, exogamous clans and had a kinship system similar to that we have described for the tribes of the Southeast, and Lowie has paid tribute to the accuracy of these pioneer observations in his own studies of the Crow Indians.

Morgan therefore never discovered the important fact that the central High Plains tribes were not organized in terms of clans—with the sole exception of the Crow. He mistook the named bands of the Blackfoot and Gros Ventre for clan groups, a mistake that later professional anthropologists, such as Kroeber and Wissler, were to repeat. He never realized that all these groups were organized in terms of bilateral descent and generation and that all cousins were classified as "brothers" and "sisters"; it is interesting to speculate what would have happened to his evolutionary formulations if he had known these facts. For Morgan came to believe that sibling terms were originally used for cross-cousins in accordance with life in the "communal family" but that, with the advent of clan exogamy, separate cross-cousin terms were developed.

The Cheyenne and Arapaho data would have confirmed his ideas with regard to the influence of clans on kinship terminology but would have forced him either to modify his major stages of social evolution or to place the clanless Cheyenne and their neighbors as intermediate between the Malayan and Ganowanian systems. When Morgan later noted the use of sibling terms for cross-cousins among the Gros Ventre, he merely said: "This last classification is not in accordance with the principles of the system" (1871: 227). Beyond the Rockies were dozens of as yet unknown tribes that did not conform to the "classificatory" system either, but Morgan had no way of knowing of them.

If we now look at the tribes of the High Plains in terms of the problems they faced, with regard both to subsistence and to competition with their neighbors, we can see their social systems in new perspective. Plains life required a flexible type of organization that could adjust both to the seasonally varying habits of the buffalo and to the requirements of protection and warfare. The amorphous and composite bands were well adapted for such purposes and could change in size and leadership as the situation demanded. A successful leader attracted new members, while those of a poor leader were lost or melted away.

In warfare, as well as in hunting, the cooperation of "brothers" was essential to survival, and I have argued elsewhere (1937: 93 ff.) that the extensions of this relationship to distant cousins, as well as to "friends" and companions in the warrior societies, was intelligible on this basis. And the principle of the "equivalence of siblings," or the "solidarity and unity of the sibling group," as Radcliffe-Brown phrased it, is basic to the understanding of much of High Plains social life. Some of the Blackfoot tribes even extended sibling terms to all relatives who were age-mates, regardless of genealogical position. And the Dakota, moving into the High Plains from the Minnesota region, came to treat their cross-cousins as if they were "siblings," so far as social behavior was concerned.

IV

We can now turn our attention to the village-dwelling tribes of the Prairie Plains and see them in better perspective. The tribes of the Missouri River region lived for the most part in semi-permanent villages composed of earth lodges and situated along tributary streams. While they participated in communal buffalo hunts during the summer and waged war on the Plain's pattern, they had a dual subsistence base and a much more elaborate social structure. Women were responsible for cultivating corn, beans, and squash in the fertile bottom lands along the streams, and the surplus was stored in large pits for winter consumption or used for trade with High Plains groups. Men hunted buffalo and other game and were responsible for protection and defense.

The tribes of the Missouri River were organized mainly in terms of unilineal descent, but there were some important differences. The Mandan and Hidatsa in the northern part were divided into matrilineal clans, which were grouped into dual divisions or moieties, and it is highly probable that the neighboring Pawnee and Arikara were once so organized, though named clans have disappeared. The Central Siouans farther south—the Omaha, Ponca, Osage, Kansa, Iowa, Oto, and related groups—were organized in terms of patrilineal clans, usually grouped into moieties or dual divisions. These clans, whether patrilineal or matrilineal, regulated marriage but had a considerable number of other functions as well. They usually owned a stock of personal names that were bestowed on individuals, they frequently controlled political or ritual positions, they had symbolic relationships to some aspect of nature, and they often had ritual duties to perform in the ceremonial calendar. In addition, there were various associations centering on war and curing, some of which were age-graded and all of which were involved in the great tribal ceremonies.

Residence in the earth-lodge villages was generally matrilocal, regardless of the formal pattern of descent, the husband coming to live with his wife and her relatives in a multi-family structure. The earth lodges were large and well built, lasting for several generations, and the associated gardens were cultivated in common by the women of the household. After the fields had been planted, the able-bodied men and their wives prepared to go on the summer communal hunt, leaving the older people and the children to look after the village and crops. During the summer hunt they traveled with tipis and camped in a camp circle, like their Plains neighbors. For the Omaha, and some of their neighbors, the camp circle directly reflected the social structure of the tribe, the clans of one moiety having fixed positions in the northern half and being symbolically associated with the sky, and the clans of the other moiety being arranged in the southern half and symbolically associated with the earth. This was accomplished by patrilocal residence, a man and his wife or wives camping with his clan mates, an organization that facilitated both hunting and defense against enemy attacks.

After a series of successful "surrounds" the hunt group returned home with the surplus buffalo meat, which had been dried and made into pemmican and which was then stored for the winter months. Smaller groups went out hunting during the fall and winter months for briefer periods, but their organization varied. In the spring the fields were cleared for planting and the annual cycle started over again.

The kinship systems of the Prairie Plains tribes were organized in terms of the "lineage principle," the Mandan, Hidatsa, Pawnee, and (probably) the Arikara having variants of the "Crow" system, and the Omaha, Ponca, Kansa, Iowa, Oto, and related groups having the "Omaha" system. Here the basic principle is that the kinship terminology is organized "vertically," in terms of the descent pattern, and that certain classes of relatives are grouped with reference to the lineage and clan, regardless of generation.

This type of system is consonant with unilateral descent, but only a limited number of tribes with a clan organization have "Crow" and "Omaha" systems. Hence Lowie and others have looked for additional factors, such as secondary marriages with the wife's brother's daughter or the mother's brother's wife, to account for the patterns of kinship terminology. But these specific marriage patterns may themselves be a function of the social structure: once an Omaha tribesman marries, he can take as a second wife any woman cf his wife's patrilineage, including his wife's brother's daughter.

The answer to this problem apparently lies in the

degree to which the clan is a "corporate" group. When the clan has a head, owns property in common, controls status positions, and is responsible for ceremonial activities, it is more likely to conceive of itself as a self-conscious group, concerned with its continuity and privileges, and may result in its being treated as a unit for various purposes, including kinship. The apparent exceptions to such a hypothesis need explanation, and we shall examine the Iroquois briefly in the next chapter when we consider the central Algonkian tribes of the Great Lakes region.

We can now see more clearly why the initial formulation of the Plains culture area was criticized by Franz Boas and others as not conforming to the distribution of social organization. If we concentrate our attention on sociocultural wholes, it is apparent that the High Plains and Prairie Plains tribes are distinctive with regard to almost all aspects of their social structure. And it is also clear that the Prairie Plains is in no sense "marginal" with regard to its social system. On the contrary, it is much more elaborate and specialized, and tribal integration is much more complex and rigid. Thus Robert H. Lowie, in his *Indians of the Plains* (1954), confuses rather than clarifies our conception of the Plains when he rejects Kroeber's separation of the Plains and Prairie areas, arguing:

These tribes share a sufficiently large number of cultural traits to be classed together as representing a distinctive mode of life. Inasmuch as they inhabit a continuous territory, it is proper to speak of a "Plains" culture area, using the geographical term in its wider sense [p. 5].

As Clyde Kluckhohn has emphasized in another connection, the greatest advance in contemporary anthropological theory is probably the increasing recognition that there is something more to culture than artifacts, linguistic texts, and lists of atomized traits. For our present purposes the added factor is structure or organization.

A brief comparison of the major orientations of the two regions should illuminate the contrasts. Thus tribal organization in the High Plains centered on the band and camp circle, with a seasonal variation related to ecological factors, whereas in the Prairie Plains the village was central and the camp circle was used only for hunting excursions during the summer. The High Plains bands were bilateral and composite, with a fixed position in the camp circle but otherwise little differentiated. The Prairie Plains village was based on a clan-moiety organization with differentiated "corporate" functions related to the tribal whole.

The subsistence activities of the High Plains centered on hunting, and raiding for horses, and the tribe had no fixed center but moved around in a claimed territory. There were seasonal surpluses, but subsistence was precarious. The village tribes, on the other hand, depended on agriculture as well as hunting and were largely sedentary. Surplus food normally was available, and trading relations were well established with High Plains groups.

Political organization in the High Plains varied but usually consisted of a council of chiefs who had achieved their status by successful war exploits and who maintained their position by successful leadership. The chiefs of the village tribes were more often hereditary, with ascribed status, though war leaders were chosen on the basis of ability. War, to begin with, was primarily defensive, but the groups that did not respond to harrassment were often wiped out.

The social structures were also quite different. The amorphous bands of the High Plains might vary in size and composition, depending on their success in hunting and war. The clan-moiety system, on the other hand, was relatively rigid and changed its composition only slowly. In the High Plains, kinship was bilateral and widely extended on the basis of generation; in the villages, kinship was unilateral and extended "vertically," as well as by means of clan relationships. The corporate possessions in the Plains belonged, for the most part, to the tribe and were often in charge of hereditary keepers, though the associations had certain corporate functions. Continuity from generation to generation was little emphasized, inheritance not being important, except in later periods for horses. The village-dwelling tribes organized their corporate activities in terms of clans and households, with both land and ritual possessions being important in inheritance.

The social structures of the High Plains tribes, in summary, were flexible and could adapt to the changing ecological conditions by breaking up or recombining. The tribal organization was loosely integrated, but unity was maintained both by external pressures and by the performance of group rituals, as well as by the greater efficiency of communal hunts. The Prairie Plains tribes, in contrast, were characterized by more highly specialized and interlocking social structures, well adapted to sedentary agricultural life but too rigid for the uncertain life of the High Plains. Both regions utilized enlarged families as domestic units, as well as associational structures, but their roles in the larger society were somewhat different.

We can now examine some of the exceptions that we have noted but not discussed. The Crow Indians of Montana, in the High Plains, had been described by Morgan and Lowie as possessing matrilineal, exogamous clans and a "Crow" type of kinship system, though otherwise conforming to the culture patterns of their neighbors. Morgan was aware of the linguistic relationship of the Crow to the Hidatsa of the Missouri village tribes, and both tradition and modern archeology indicate that the Crow broke away and moved up the Missouri River to their present habitat before the arrival of Europeans. Here they gave up agriculture, except for the planting of tobacco, and became typical bison-hunters. In this process they had to give up their village unity and spread out over a larger territory, ultimately dividing into the River Crow and the Mountain Crow. And, while they maintained their formal clan structure, the clan groupings were modified and the clans lost much of their corporate character, though they were the nucleus of the new band organization that was being developed. Residence in the tipis was still commonly matrilocal, but prominent individuals might set up their own households with multiple wives. Morgan noted the role of the mother's brother—here classed with the older brother terminologically—as having more authority than the father in the latter's household, and clearly described matrilineal succession to the office of chief and matrilineal inheritance of property.

The kinship system was also modified in an interesting way. Lowie's later researches indicate that the basic "Crow" pattern continued to be used for reference, but in direct address the pattern shifted to a "generation" type very similar to that of the High Plains tribes. Thus the father's sister was addressed as "mother" and her children were "brothers" and "sisters" rather than "fathers" and "father's sisters." Morgan recorded a variant pattern, with the father's sister and her female descendants being classed with the "mother," which may be an intermediate stage (as in the Choctaw sequence of Spoehr) or a result of mixing referential and vocative usages, of which Morgan was as yet unaware. Lowie, in comparing the Hidatsa and Crow terminologies in detail, asks (1917: 342): "What sociological reason could conceivably be adduced to account for the classification of the same relative with the mother in direct address and as distinct from the mother in non-vocative terminology?" He goes on to state: "Here once more we are obviously dealing with a linguistic phenomenon." But if we look at the vocative and referential subsystems in the light of the broader perspectives we have been sketching, it is clear that sociological factors have been at work and that the Crow are a village tribe in the midst of the process of adjusting to Plains conditions. This is not a question of simple borrowing; the Crow are losing their clan system, and the kinship system is being changed in terms of new groupings for social action. We think of vocative terms as more sensitive to new conditions because they involve face-to-face relations, while terms of reference are usually more conservative.

A parallel set of changes, which has gone even further, can be seen in the case of the Wichita and their Caddoan-speaking relatives in the Prairie Plains. The Wichita today have a social system typical of the High Plains, but Karl and Iva Schmitt (1952) have adduced evidence for a shift from a matrilineal type of social structure with Crow kinship patterns to a bilateral, generational type of social system, paralleling that found by Spoehr for the Southeast, and also similar to what we have just suggested for the Crow Indians themselves. The Pawnee have matrilineal descent, but related in historic times to villages rather than clans, and a modified Crow type of kinship.[3] The Arikara, their close relatives, seem to have been changing in the same direction but were practically wiped out by smallpox before they could be adequately studied. Recent supporting evidence comes from archeology, where James Deetz (in his Ph.D. dissertation in 1960) confirms the Schmitts's hypothesis in terms of the changing association of pottery stylistic attributes over time in household assemblages and concludes: "Finding themselves in a new and different area and beset by troubles, the Arikara began to change their social structure away from the Crow type to a more generationally based system, better suited to meet the effects of rapidly changing conditions."

The case of the eastern Shoshone and Comanche is at the opposite extreme. Here Julian Steward (1938) has shown how the horse enabled small hunting and gathering groups in the Great Basin to come together in larger bands and ultimately move into the plains. The Comanche became the most notable tribe in the southern High Plains and, with their great horse herds, approximated to a pastoral group. But their social organization lagged somewhat behind. Their bands sometimes expanded into sub-tribes, but they never developed the camp circle or associational structures. And they adopted the Sun Dance only in 1874 in a desperate effort to unite the tribe in a time of crisis. The kinship system came to approximate the High Plains model, though there were survivals of Basin terminological forms, and they continued to practice certain unique forms of marriage. S. C. Oliver (1962: 71–76) has discussed the reasons why the Comanche

[3] Gene Weltfish, in *The Lost Universe* (1965), has provided us with much additional information on Pawnee social organization, including the practice of avunculocal residence, in which a boy was sent to live with his maternal uncle for instruction.

failed to become "typical" in these respects and concludes that both the somewhat different ecology of the southern plains and the Great Basin cultural heritage were involved. As Wallace and Hoebel have put it: "The Comanche band was strikingly similar in organization to the aboriginal Shoshonean groups of the Great Basin in the days preceding the horse" (1952: 22).

These instances tell us something about social structures and their relevance to different environments and styles of life. The specialized clan-moiety structures of the Prairie Plains were developed in connection with relatively stable life, based in part on agriculture. The matrilocal extended families of the earth lodges facilitated the cultivation of crops by women and are consonant with matrilineal descent, as practiced by the northern village groups. The central Siouans apparently came into the Prairie Plains relatively late and borrowed the earth-lodge complex. The latter is relatively old in the Prairie Plains and was even more widespread in late prehistoric and protohistoric times, and certain of the large archeological earth-lodge cultures were ancestral to the historic Pawnee. It is possible that the Omaha and their neighbors came in from the Middle Mississippi archeological region with a patrilineally oriented system; Mathews' linguistic reconstruction of a possible ancestral "Omaha" kinship terminology would support this inference. They continued—or developed—matrilocal extended families for the earth-lodge community but expressed their patrilineal clan-moiety structure during the summer hunts, when they camped in a circle in terms of patrilocal groupings. If this reconstruction is correct, the alterations of residence noted by Reo Fortune (1932: 24) reflect the different *organizations* for subsistence activities rather than being the initiators of change in the social system. The dual life might ultimately have given rise to a system of double descent, with the recognition of the shallow matrilineages in the earth lodge, but there is no evidence for the latter.

When these specialized and highly integrated societies moved out on the High Plains permanently and gave up agriculture in favor of the greater rewards and excitement of buffalo-hunting, which came with the introduction of the horse, they developed a more flexible social organization to adjust to the varying ecological conditions and to protect them from neighboring groups. The band organization and the widely extended "generational" kinship provided such a loosely integrated society, which could suffer serious losses and yet reform. Some groups, such as the Omaha and Pawnee, tried to maintain both ways of life; others, such as the Crow and Wichita, went all the way. On the other side, Shoshonean-speaking groups moving into the plains had to build up their simple structure in order to compete in the plains environment and stay alive.

Athabaskan-speaking groups from southern Canada once played an important role in the southern High Plains, but they were partly exterminated by their neighbors with better weapons or organization. Some remnants, such as the Chiricahua and Lipan Apache, and possibly the Jicarilla, moved into marginal areas and exploited new ecological niches. Others, such as the Kiowa-Apache and the Sarsi, joined larger groups or federations and thus maintained their society. Still other tribes from the Rocky Mountain and Plateau regions made periodic excursions to the plains for buffalo hunting, often going in large intertribal "task forces" (Anastasio, n.d.) for protection against the plains-dwelling tribes. These groups acquired a superficial overlay of Plains traits, in terms of costume and horse culture, but maintained their Plateau style of organization and ritual.

V

In broad historical perspective the Plains area has gone through a number of phases. At the end of the last glaciation, some ten or twelve thousand years ago, the central and southern plains were occupied by Paleo-Indian hunters of large game, particularly mammoths, bison, wild horses, camels, and other fauna now extinct. These Clovis and Folsom hunters, whom we know as yet only from their camp and "kill" sites, gradually improved their weapons and skills, but the altithermal period brought extensive droughts, driving early man and animals from the plains and apparently bringing about the extinction of the pleistocene fauna that had survived. Later, with an amelioration of the climate, the plains were gradually repopulated with a smaller species of bison that had survived on the margins or in the forest areas to the north and east.

During the succeeding periods the plains seems to have been intermittently occupied by horticultural groups extending out along the tributary bottom lands from the Missouri valley and by trade or settlements from the southwest across the southern plains. Earth lodges made their appearance, the earlier communities being small and scattered and the later ones larger and organized for defense. The evidence for nomadic life is more difficult to trace but is present in camp sites and tipi rings. The Plains tribes discovered by Coronado were both nomadic buffalo hunters who had mastered life on the staked plains and village-dwelling horticulturists farther east living in grass huts much like the later Wichita.

Francis Haines has traced the spread of the horse northward, from the Spanish settlements in New Mexico, where it reached the eastern Shoshone around A.D 1700 and had spread to most of the Plains groups by A.D. 1750. It is clear that the horse both intensified the type of life described by Coronado for the High Plains, through replacing the dog and making hunting and raiding more profitable, and revolutionized values in the marginal Prairie Plains by offering new opportunities to sedentary horticulturists.

The modern tribes of the High Plains, with one or two exceptions, are relatively new to the area. The Athabaskan-speaking groups began to move southward from Canada some six hundred years ago and gradually split up to form the various Apache and Navaho tribes and almost completely remodeled their cultural patterns in the process. In the northeast the French had armed their Indian allies, and the Ojibwa gradually forced the Dakota westward out of Minnesota and onto the plains. In this process the Cheyenne were also forced westward, and Morgan was told that they formerly lived at the great bend of the Cheyenne River, a tributary of the Red River of the North, where their abandoned earth-lodge village was still traceable. They moved across the Missouri near the end of the eighteenth century and within a few generations were judged one of the most typical of High Plains tribes.

This historical data was "forgotten" in the 1920's under Wissler's conception of the Plains culture as "timeless" and

developed *in situ,* and Grinnell's statements from old
Cheyenne informants as to former matrilineal descent and
horticultural practices were discounted, until Duncan
Strong's excavations in the 1930's re-established the Cheyenne as a former village-dwelling tribe. Other Algonkian-
speaking groups, the Arapaho, Gros Ventre, Blackfoot,
Plains Cree, and Plains Ojibwa, all came into the northern
plains from the east or northeast, also in relatively recent
times. The Comanche, on the other hand, represent one
of the eastern Shoshone bands that early secured horses
and moved southward into the Texas plains. Among the
High Plains tribes only the Kiowa cannot be traced to an
outside area; their closest linguistic relatives are the
Tanoan-speaking pueblos of the Rio Grande.

In my earlier study of the Cheyenne and Arapaho I
noted that "tribes coming into the Plains with *different*
backgrounds and social systems ended up with *similar*
kinship systems" (1937:93). I think it is now clear that
they achieved a common pattern of social structure as
well. Wissler's explanation of the culture pattern as the
result of a mechanical process of diffusion and borrowing
is far too simple an answer for the processes we have been
outlining. The complex interrelations between technology,
the environment, and the social structure provide an ecological explanation that is more satisfying, if less simple.

In evolutionary perspective the move to the High
Plains would be culturally "regressive" for most groups.
But the horse opened up possibilities for raiding and warfare that had a strong appeal to the male population,
and the apparently inexhaustible supply of buffalo made
subsistence seemingly secure. Defeat at the hands of
United States forces and the establishment of reservations,

coupled with the sudden disappearance of the great buffalo herds, led to a traumatic period. Tribes once agricultural found it difficult to revert to farming or develop a role in modern life. There were both uprisings and the development of "nativistic" movements, such as the Ghost Dance. Ultimately, the Peyote cult took the place of much of the older ritual, though the Sun Dance continues to be performed by a few tribes. At the modern "powwows" they still dress and dance as "braves," but, as Gordon McGregor has remarked, "they are warriors without weapons."

VI

Not all the village-dwelling tribes of the Prairie Plains moved westward. The Mandan and Hidatsa, small Siouan-speaking tribes in the Missouri River region, had long lived in the region in earth-lodge communities practicing agriculture in the bottom lands and hunting on the prairie. Smallpox epidemics in the early nineteenth century decimated both groups, and the survivors were established in a single village about 1862, along with a few Arikara. Later, after allotment of their lands, they lived scattered in a number of small communities on the Fort Berthold reservation.

Both tribes were originally organized in terms of matrilineal clans and moieties, a set of societies, and a Crow-type kinship system. Edward Bruner went to study Lone Hill, one of the Mandan-Hidatsa communities, in the early 1950's, in part to see whether the same progressive changes in Crow-type kinship systems under white acculturation had also taken place there. Much to his surprise, he found a quite different process to be dominant: an abrupt change or "mutation" to a white model, with no apparent intermediate stages.

Lone Hill, a relatively isolated and small community, had a total population of some 267 Indians living in 48 nuclear families in 1951. Hidatsa is the dominant language, but the great majority also knew some English. Bruner (1955: 840–50) found that the majority of the population still used a Crow kinship terminology—essentially similar to that recorded by Morgan almost a century earlier. But he also found a smaller number of families who employed an American type of system, with English terms. Furthermore, there was little or no evidence for the transitional systems outlined by Spoehr (1947) for the tribes of the Southeast.

Bruner (1955: 845) has, therefore, suggested two distinct processes involved in kinship change: (1) slow modification over several generations through an orderly and progressive shift in type and (2) a more radical change indicated by an abrupt shift from one type of system to another. He finds evidence for both types in the Southeast and in the Mandan-Hidatsa, but the relative importance of each is considerably different.

In examining acculturation in Lone Hill, Bruner (1956) found much evidence of cultural admixture, but the basic contrast was in terms of orientation toward Indian values or white values. And, in studying the families who had shifted to the American generational system, he found in each case that there had been an Indian-white marriage in the family in recent generations. He concludes:

The presence of the white generational system in Lone Hill is due to neither cultural "borrowing," adult learning, nor rearrangements in the social structure precipitated by new conditions. Individuals in Lone Hill learn the American kinship system in the English language within the intimate domestic situation [1955: 846].

Not all the families with a white ancestor in recent generations have made this shift, but the presence of a white model is a crucial factor. Among the "unacculturated" families a white model was absent in thirty-one families and present in only three; among the seven "acculturated" and seven marginal families a white model was present in all instances.

The "acculturated" and "unacculturated" families are characterized by considerable hostility and little interaction, and they form the nucleus of the "progressive" and "conservative" factions. Bruner, in analyzing the processes that have resulted in these two subsocieties suggests that "the differences in degree of acculturation found among the Indian peoples are in large measure a product of early experience in the intimate family group, and the cultural orientation of their parents or surrogates" (1956: 605).

Here, then, is another important process by which social systems may change and which needs to be taken into account in all cases of acculturation when intermarriage takes place. The new model may be Indian or white, but must consciously wish to instill the values and practices of his reference group. Bruner (1955: 844–45) cites the case of a mixed Hidatsa-Arikara marriage in which the child was taught to call his Hidatsa relatives by one pattern and his Arikara relatives by a different pattern.

VII

We have seen that Lewis H. Morgan's four field trips to the Missouri River region initiated the comparative study of social systems and represented the first organized attempt to answer specific questions through planned research. In contrast to his Iroquois research, where he had spent several years getting a more rounded picture of one tribe, he here secured selected information on kinship terminology and clan organization, along with miscellaneous information, on a large number of tribal groups but without the opportunity to see very much of the society and culture in which they were embedded. Even so, his data are surprisingly accurate and give us a base for compartive studies and for studies of social and cultural change.

We have also seen that his broad, functional view of society, and his interest in history and development, can now be carried much further than he was able to do. By paying attention to the variants that he lumped together, by seeing the environment in dynamic relationship to sociocultural life, and by looking at the High Plains in both historical and functional perspective, we can better evaluate the role of social structures. Social structures have jobs to do, and, when the tasks change, specialized structures may be inefficient and must be able to adapt to new conditions if the society is to maintain itself. Morgan saw this macroscopically in terms of broad stages. Modern social anthropology has made its greatest progress by examining structure and function microscopically —within the tribe and region. But without Morgan's pioneer efforts we would not be able to carry our analysis nearly so far. His tables give data that are no longer available for many tribes and they are given in a form that is usable for many new purposes. And more sophisticated linguistic analyses, such as Floyd Lounsbury's "A Semantic Analysis of the Pawnee Kinship Usage" (1956) go back to Morgan's data.

IV

THE OJIBWA AND THE INDIANS
OF THE GREAT LAKES REGION:
THE ROLE OF CROSS-COUSIN
MARRIAGE[1]

I

WHEN LEWIS H. MORGAN DISCOVERED, IN 1858, THAT THE
Algonkian-speaking Ojibwa, residing on the southern
shores of Lake Superior, had a pattern of grouping relatives almost identical with that of the Iroquoian-speaking
Seneca of New York State, he initiated a comparative
study of kinship terminology of which we have already
seen some of the results with regard to the Indians of the
Southeast and those of the Plains region. Now let us return to the Ojibwa and their neighbors in the Great Lakes
area to see what we have been able to add to Morgan's
pioneer contributions in this important region.

The Great Lakes had been the major avenue of entry
into the interior of North America during the seventeenth
and eighteenth centuries and thus have played an important role in the history of this continent. The development
of the fur trade and the struggle between the French and

[1] I have utilized several sections of my "Social Anthropology: Methods and Results" (1955) relating to the analysis of cross-cousin marriage
in the Great Lakes region, incorporating whole paragraphs here and
there without special citation. For this region the studies of Speck,
Cooper, and Hallowell are indispensable, and the whole area is well
covered in Frederick Johnson (ed.), *Man in Northeastern North America*
(1946).

English for control of the waterways involved Indian groups as both pawns and allies and resulted in religious acculturation and economic dependence as well as in internecine war and tribal disintegration. In Morgan's time most of the Algonkian-speaking tribes of the Atlantic region were either extinct or removed to reservations beyond the Mississippi, and only the Iroquois and a few other groups still occupied fragments of their aboriginal homeland.

North of the St. Lawrence–Great Lakes region, however, the changes were more gradual, and it is possible to see the ecological conditions under which various groups lived and to evaluate the effects of the fur trade and the introduction of the trading-post economy. In addition, we shall attempt to assess the significance of an added factor: the role of cross-cousin marriage. Morgan's famous stages of social evolution depended essentially upon broad changes in marriage patterns: from promiscuity, through group regulation, to monogamy; and he thought of all the American Indians as essentially at the stage at which marriage is controlled by clan exogamy. And, while he was familiar with such customs as the sororate and levirate, the preferential or prescriptive regulation of marriage with certain classes of cousins was not yet conceptualized. Not until Edward B. Tylor's famous essay "On a Method of Investigating the Development of Institutions" (1889) was the significance of "cross-cousin marriage," as Tylor called the custom in which the children of a brother married the children of his sister, recognized in social anthropology.

Hence, when the women of a Cree family from Pembina on the Red River of the North told Morgan that "cousins marry among the Crees" (1959: 111) and attempted to explain the situation on the Saskatchewan, he failed to clarify these statements or follow them up, though they contained an important key to our understanding of the social systems of the northern Algonkian-speaking peoples. Later, in discussing the Dravidian systems of South India, he noted that the few differences between them and the Seneca Iroquois might be the result of marriage: "Unless I cohabit with all my female cousins, and am excluded from cohabiting with the wives of my male cousins, these relationships can't be explained from the nature of descents" (1871: 486). But this mode to understanding has only been clarified since the work of Rivers and later social anthropologists. We shall see that it is crucial, not only to the interpretation of the kinship systems of the northern Algonkians, but to those of the Dakota groups that we met in the previous chapter, and possibly even to the Iroquois systems as well.

II

Northeastern North America, particularly the region north of the Great Lakes and east of Lake Winnipeg, has long been considered a region with a distinctive culture. The early scholars, such as Frank Speck, who first mapped the band territories and described their culture, considered the Northeast as a "refuge" area, occupied by peoples who were adjusted to boreal life and whose culture represented that of the first migrants to the New World. But we now know (Quimby 1960) that most of this region was long occupied by ice masses and glacial lakes and did not become suitable for habitation until sometime after 3000 B.C. Hence, while there are numerous evidences of paleo-

Indian remains south of the Great Lakes, mostly in the form of Clovis fluted points, which were apparently used to hunt mastodons and other large game, the migrants into the Canadian Shield were relatively late and had already developed rather complex cultures.

With the Eskimo of the Hudson Bay and Labrador coastal regions we will not be here concerned. They represent an expansion of Thule-type Eskimos across Arctic Canada from northern Alaska, which reached the eastern area about A.D. 1300, and we have only recently begun to get adequate studies of their social structure. In general, there has been a clear distinction between Eskimo and Indian cultures, maintained both by an adjustment to different ecologies and by hostilities, though some diffusion of cultural traits has occurred in both directions.

The major populations of the interior of the Northeast spoke languages related to Central Algonkian. The Algonkian stock has a continuous distribution north of the Great Lakes and has expanded along the Atlantic as far as the Carolinas and south of the western Great Lakes as far as Kentucky or Tennessee, with outliers in the Plains and distant relatives as far away as California. Mary Haas (1958) has also recently adduced evidence for a more remote affiliation of Algonkian with the Gulf languages, including Muskogean and other groups in the Southeast. (This would have pleased Morgan, who thought that all the American Indian languages were ultimately genetically related; it may also provide a linguistic correlate to the cultural unity that Kroeber perceived for the whole eastern region of North America.)

More relevant to our purposes are the dialect divisions, since they provide evidence of more recent cultural unity. The Cree, Montagnais, and Naskapi form a dialect chain across the northern portion of the region, from which the Cree have expanded westward in historic times in connection with the fur trade. South of them, the Ojibwa, Ottawa, and Potawatomi form another dialect chain. These groups were also forced westward by the combined pressure of Iroquois warfare and European expansion and by the lure of the fur trade. The Ojibwa, originally clustered around Sault Ste Marie, were better protected than the Ottawa or Potawatomi and were able to expand both north and northwest of Lake Superior and southwest and west until they reached the Plains. In this process, which began in the late seventeenth century, they not only had to adjust to a variety of new environments but to survive the sharpened competition of their enemies as well.

South of the western Great Lakes in historic times were another series of Central Algonkian-speaking tribes more distantly related to the groups mentioned above: the Menomini near Green Bay; the Sauk and Fox, with the related Kickapoo; the Miami and Illinois confederacy tribes; and the Shawnee farther to the south. Within this region and adjacent to the Menomini were the Siouan-speaking Winnebago, whose closest relatives were the Iowa and Oto on the margins of the Prairie Plains. Further east were the Iroquois groups: the Huron and their neighbors and the Five Nations. When Cartier sailed up the St. Lawrence in 1535 he found Iroquoian-speaking groups in control of the region around Quebec. But, when Champlain established colonies in that region sixty-five years later, the "Laurentian" Iroquois had disappeared, and what happened to them is still something of a mystery.

The subsistence patterns of the northern tribes centered primarily on hunting and fishing, but horticulture became more important as one reached the Huron and their neighbors, and the more southern prairie and parkland groups in the Illinois region had a dual economy much like that of the Central Siouans. In areas of Wisconsin and northern Michigan, wild rice became an important ingredient in the economy.

The northern tribes were organized into bands, each of which was a political unit. In summer the families comprising a band would come together at some central lake or fishing spot and form a village community under the leadership of a headman—later the location was shifted to be convenient to a trading post. In the late fall the family groups scattered over the band territory, each in its own "family hunting territory." For the central tribes just north of the Great Lakes there was an added feature: a patrilineal, exogamous clan system, which acted primarily to control marriage and mourning. Farther south, the clan system was more important and developed many "corporate" functions; also, there was a dual division of the tribe, which did not control marriage but formed the basis for rivalry in games and ceremonial activities. The Iroquois nations had an even more elaborate social structure, with matrilineal clans and moieties and an overall political structure, the famous confederacy.

The ritual organization also varied from north to south. In the northern tribes the shaman was preeminent, and rituals centered on the supply of game and successful hunting, on the one hand, and the curing of illness, on the other. In the central tribes the "shamans" were organized into a medicine society called the Midewiwin, which had several ranks or degrees and which put on public performances of magic at its annual meetings. Farther south, there were societies organized around medicine bundles with secret rituals and specializations in curing and welfare ceremonies. Here, again, the Iroquois tribes were more elaborately organized, with an annual ceremonial calendar climaxed by a great midwinter festival.

The variations from north to south were in part a function of ecological determinants. The crucial season for survival in the north is the winter, and the winter grouping was closely correlated with the habits and numbers of the game animals on which the populations depended. Among the northern Naskapi, where primary dependence was on the migratory caribou, or wild reindeer, small bands of 30–50 members remained together, for the most part, during the winter, relying on surpluses secured by the autumn hunt and on fishing through the ice. To the south, the bands depended on sedentary game and broke up during the fall and winter in terms of hunting tracts, which were protected by trespass rules and game conservation. These tracts were exploited by extended families, either a man and his sons, or a man and his sons-in-law, or a set of brothers and their families. This system of "family hunting territories" allowed a denser population than was found farther north and provided two adult males, the most efficient number for proper exploitation of a territory. The system was long thought to be aboriginal in its rules of trespass and clear-cut property boundaries, but is now thought to have been a reflex of the fur trade, with its greater emphasis upon beaver skins and other furs. Today, in much of Canada the trapping territories are mapped, registered, and patroled by the government.

Where horticulture was practiced, generally south of the present border, denser populations were possible, and semi-permanent villages, with various combinations of agriculture—or wild-rice gathering—and hunting developed. Much of this life around the southern and western Great Lakes was greatly modified in the seventeenth century by Iroquois raids all the way to the Mississippi, which concentrated numerous groups to the west of Lake Michigan.

There is both a sociological and an ecological gradient from the northeast to the southwest of the northern area, which involves the interrelationship of several factors: (1) the productivity of the natural environment, (2) the definiteness of the local organization, (3) the degree of band cohesion, (4) the strength of patrilineal tendencies, and (5) the frequency of extended family units. The size and composition of the winter hunting groups, the size of the hunting tracts, and the rules governing their transfer, all are closely related to specific ecological conditions (Arch Cooper, n.d.).

III

On his field trips to the Missouri region Morgan gathered some sixteen kinship schedules for the Algonkian-speaking tribes and nine for the Dakota and other Siouan groups. During 1861, on a journey to Pembina and Fort Garry on the Red River of the North, he acquired a considerable amount of information on the Cree and Ojibwa, as well as a glimpse into the lives of the northern Athabaskans of the Mackenzie region and the local mixed-blood communities along the Red River (He also discovered sound shifts among the Cree and other dialects: "The permutations of consonants in Indian languages . . . may be governed by a law equivalent to that discovered by Grimm in the Indo-European Languages" [1959: 117].)

We have seen that Morgan failed to follow up the possible significance of the marriage of cousins among the Cree and their neighbors. That honor belongs to W. H. R. Rivers, who initiated the modern theoretical study of cross-cousin marriage systems. As a result of working with such systems in India and Melanesia, Rivers returned to Morgan's hypothesis that there is a close connection between methods of denoting relationship and forms of social organization, including those based on different varieties of the institution of marriage. Rivers, on the basis of Morgan's schedules, suggested (in 1914) the possibility that cross-cousin marriage formerly existed among some of the northern Athabaskans, the Cree, and certain of the Dakota tribes, but American anthropologists in general dismissed this suggestion as unwarranted, since cross-cousin marriage had not been reported for more than a very few New World groups.

However, A. I. Hallowell's discovery (1930) that the kinship terms recorded in early documents reflected cross-cousin marriage among the Ojibwa, Ottawa, and Algonkin, and W. D. Strong's discovery (1929) of cross-cousin marriage in full operation among the northern bands of the Naskapi in Labrador, stimulated further inquiry during the 1930's and resulted in widespread evidence for the present or recent practice of cross-cousin marriage among the northern Algonkians.

I have discussed the significance of cross-cousin marriage for the Northeast in some detail elsewhere (1955). Briefly, the practice of systematically marrying someone in the social category of cross-cousin results in a kinship system in which relatives by marriage are normally consanguineal relatives. Thus one's father-in-law is already a "mother's brother" and one's mother-in-law is a "father's sister," so a separate set of affinal terms is not necessary. It was by noting these equivalences that Rivers was able to predict the occurrence of cross-cousin marriage among the Cree and other groups. We can also see that the practice of marrying a cross-cousin—a "father's sister's daughter" or a "mother's brother's daughter"—is one way of solving the incest problem in small groups. Marriage within the elementary family is forbidden almost everywhere for both psychological and sociological reasons, and these restrictions are generally extended to the children of two brothers or of two sisters—or of parallel cousins. But marriage has to take place with someone, and, in small isolated groups, cross-cousin marriage is a custom that permits social life to continue with relatively little disruption.

Marriage is also an instrument for alliance as well as an individual concern. As such it may be used to knit the members of a community more tightly together or to ally families with neighboring or adjacent groups. The Cree and northern Ojibwa view their own kinship system as made up of two categories: (1) kinsmen or relatives, including the "father's brothers" and "mother's sisters" and their children, and (2) cognates and affines, including the "father's sisters" and "mother's brothers" and their families. The latter are considered "non-relatives" for marriage purposes, and they have different expectable behavior patterns and structural positions in the social system, even though both groups may be descended from common grandparents and thus genealogically related.

Cross-cousin marriage, when practiced in small bilatterally organized bands, creates a social structure of its own. Thus, the northern Naskapi bands, as described by

Strong, represent a distinctive type of social structure: a bilateral band held together by cross-cousin marriage. There was some intermarriage with neighboring bands, but the extremely low population density (one person per 300 square miles) made band interaction proportionately rare. Farther to the south, among the Montagnais bands, where the population density was one person per 25 square miles, there was a correlative increase in band size and a reduction in the size of hunting territories. Cross-cousin marriage once operated here in a more complex fashion, but three hundred years of religious acculturation make it difficult to reconstruct the details.

Among the more isolated northern Ojibwa of the Berens River region, however, Hallowell (1937) found the practice of cross-cousin marriage in full operation and was able to show how the system operates. All the characteristic terminological equations of cross-cousin marriage were found, and the kinship system not only defines the social status of individuals in such a way that only persons of the same generation are potential mates but divides this generation into "siblings," whom one cannot marry, and "cross-cousins," who are potential mates. Further, marriages that do not fit this pattern are treated as if they do, so far as the application of kinship terms is concerned. The Ojibwa have a patrilineal clan system as well, which further regulates marriage through clan exogamy and the sororate and levirate and serves for hospitality and tribal integration. Strangers of one's own clan and generation are classed as "siblings"; all other clanspeople are treated as affinal relatives and "cross-cousins," or potential mates.

The first important studies of social change with regard to the northern tribes were carried out by Strong and Hallowell. Duncan Strong (1929) found that the Davis Inlet band, just to the south of the Barren Ground band of Naskapi, did not practice cross-cousin marriage, though their language and culture was otherwise almost identical. Further, a detailed comparison of their kinship terminologies showed interesting changes: the cross-cousins were classed as "siblings" by the Davis Inlet people rather than as "cross-cousins." In both groups the relations between brother and sister were marked by reserve and respect, but the Barren Ground band had a complex series of joking relations with cross-cousins that involved sexual relations and might lead to marriage. Among the Davis Inlet band this joking behavior was restricted to "siblings-in-law," who were still prospective mates under the sororate and levirate. The latter band had been under strong mission influences, which had apparently resulted in the abandonment of cross-cousin marriage and the adjustment of both kinship terminology and kinship behavior to accord with the new situation.

Hallowell, utilizing these and his own studies, concluded that the "fundamental social organization north of the Great Lakes and the St. Lawrence River was once essentially similar "to that in the Lake Winnipeg area" (1937: 108) and that the contemporary variations in kinship and marriage practices were "intelligible as variants of a basic pattern that had undergone modification as a result of acculturative processes and differences in local conditions." This working hypothesis has proved of great importance, as we shall see.

Ruth Landes was also carrying out field studies of the Ojibwa in the middle 1930's and concentrated her atten-

tion on the groups on either side of the border in the
Rainy Lake region of southwestern Ontario. She found
the Canadian Ojibwa living in small villages of from three
to fifteen related families during the summer but breaking
up into individual family units, each of which exploited
its own hunting and trapping grounds, during the winter
months. Here the kinship terminology and behavior of
relatives is very similar to the Cree groups to the north
and the northern Ojibwa. Among the Canadian Ojibwa
cross-cousin marriage was still practiced, but, on the
Manitou reserve on Rainy River, she found cross-cousin
marriage to be forbidden—there was a taboo on marriage
between any relatives.

Landes noted the continuance of the same kinship
terminology and behavior practices on the Rainy River
reserve and thought the abandonment of cross-cousin
marriage to be a recent development as a consequence of
contact with the Dakota Sioux. Her *Ojibwa Sociology*
(1937) was in press at the time Hallowell presented his
hypotheses, so she did not consider the possibility of
acculturative pressures from white society or, alternately,
the effects of larger concentrations of population on the
reserves as factors in the giving-up of cross-cousin
marriage.

An opportunity to test these hypotheses was provided
by the Red Lake Ojibwa, who are related to those at
Rainy Lake and elsewhere and who have been subject to
greater acculturation on their reserve in northern Minnesota. Here, where cross-cousin marriage is no longer practiced, Elizabeth Bott (n.d.) found that the kinship
terminology still reflects the cross-cousin marriage equivalences, but the behavior patterns between relatives have

changed. Thus a cross-cousin was said to be "just like a sister or brother," and marriage with them was viewed with horror. Relatives were counted as far as third cousins, and marriage should take place beyond that range. Further, the joking patterns no longer took place with cross-cousins, but only with siblings-in-law. Bott also found the patrilineal clan system in operation, with patrilocal residence and inheritance in the patrilineal line, and a more settled and concentrated pattern of life than among the Canadian groups.

This preliminary comparison of the Ojibwa groups suggests that the kinship system is, in this case also, a rather sensitive indicator of social and cultural change. All these groups had a common cultural ancestry in the seventeenth century, centered on the region adjacent to Sault Ste Marie, from which some moved northwest and others south and west. Hallowell's hypothesis allows us to see them as variant expressions of similar acculturative processes and possibly also of ecological factors. From north to south among the Ojibwa we have, first, a fully developed cross-cousin marriage system, then the same terminological and behavioral system without cross-cousin marriage, and, finally, a system in which the behavior patterns begin to change but the terminology remains the same. We can predict that cross-cousins will soon be differentiated from siblings-in-law, as well. This differentiation is an important marker in the breakdown of cross-cousin marriage systems, as we have noted for the Naskapi.

IV

We can now extend our comparisons in a number of directions. Thus some of the western Cree groups early moved out onto the northern margins of the Plains, to be followed later by the Plains Ojibwa. David Mandelbaum, who has described the Plains Cree (1940), found them occupying the transitional area between the forests and the plains. They were organized in large bilateral bands that were loose territorial units organized around a chief and his relatives. The kinship system is organized in terms of cross-cousin marriage, but there are alternative terms for various relatives-in-law. Cross-cousin marriage was reported for some of the easternmost bands but was not practiced by those farther out on the Plains. The modern system is also more "classificatory" than that earlier recorded by Morgan, which also reflected cross-cousin marriage in its terminological equations. Hallowell was told by the resident priest on the Hobbema Reserve in Alberta that marriages of second cousins had a high incidence among the Plains Cree residing there but that the marriage of first cousins was extremely rare.

The Plains Ojibwa (cf. Howard 1963–64) were later migrants into the prairie region, but by the 1790's small groups of Ojibwa had reached the Red River and became hunters for the trading posts in association with Cree and Assiniboine. They later came to occupy the Turtle Mountain region of North Dakota, as well as southern Manitoba and Saskatchewan. These Ojibwa were organized into large bands and those at Turtle Mountain hunted buffalo on the plains during the summer and returned to the mountains during the winter, when they divided into family groups. There were changes in almost all aspects of cultural life and particularly in social organization. According to Harold Scheffler (1958), the marriage of close cross-cousins came to be regarded as incestuous and all cousins were classed as "siblings" and treated as such, though the terminology suffered only minor modification. The clan system also changed, with one's own clan being a means of identifying relatives who could not be married, and other clans being treated as "non-relatives" rather than as "cross-cousins" and potential affines.

These changes reflect in part the influence of white contacts but were under way when the first Catholic missionaries arrived in the 1850's. They also reflect the influence of the series of factors concerned with the adjustment to Plains life mentioned in the previous chapter. As the Cree and Ojibwa groups moved onto the margins of the Plains, they had to adapt to new conditions of hunting and warfare, for which their old system was inadequate. Part of this shift is reflected in the increased size of the bands and in better organized warrior groups and leadership. And certain of the changes can be seen reflected in the social system: in the shift away from cross-cousin marriage to a broader-ranged generational kinship system.

From this standpoint we can now see that the Arapaho and Gros Ventre may represent the last stages of this process of adjustment to Plains conditions. For these tribes still show a few terminological equations that are reminiscent of cross-cousin marriage and that may be cognate with those of their distant Algonkian-speaking kin in the Great Lakes region. Here the structural requirements of a wider integration incident to life in a more favorable environment, and constant warfare, have been significant factors in the abandonment of cross-cousin marriage.

Harold Hickerson has made an important contribution to this problem in his recent study of the *Southwestern Chippewa* (1962). He traces these groups from their earlier residence at Sault Ste Marie along the south shore of Lake Superior, where they resided from 1679 to 1765. From there they moved south and west into northern Minnesota and Wisconsin, where they came into continued conflict with the eastern Dakota or Sioux. The Chippewa, as the Ojibwa south of the border are generally called, had better weapons, but the Dakota had larger villages and were better organized. The struggle was over hunting grounds, and, in order to succeed, the Chippewa had to develop the village as a permanent unit and to organize village alliances and warrior organizations, which were unknown in the north. Hickerson has found no reference to cross-cousin marriage for the southwestern Chippewa in the historic period and concludes that they "had long since dropped the practice of cross-cousin marriage, not through the influences attributable to simple acculturative factors but for dynamic socio-political reasons" (1962: 86).

Finally, we must mention the excellent study of R. W. Dunning, *Social and Economic Change among the Northern Ojibwa* (1959), which is the first detailed study of the structure and functioning of an Ojibwa band organization throughout its yearly cycle and in terms of the new influences from the outside world. The Pekangekum band, which he studied in 1954–55, is the most isolated of the Berens River bands studied by Hallowell in the 1930's. Dunning gives a detailed account of the ecology and the economy and their relation to the summer and winter groupings and also provides our most satisfactory account of the operation of cross-cousin marriage and the kinship system.

Of particular importance for our purposes, however, has been the effect of the "family allowances" system of the Canadian government, which has greatly increased the economic resources of the band community. Most of the band now resides permanently around the trading post, and men commute to their trapping territories. The population ceiling has been raised, and population has increased in direct proportion to the increase in subsidies. The band has also become much more endogamous than before, with most marriages taking place within the community. Further, while cross-cousin marriage is still practiced, there is a statistical shift from close cousins to more distant cousins. Here, *in situ*, so to speak, the same kinds of changes are in progress that we have noted for the groups moving out onto the plains, where the buffalo offered a more secure food supply, once the techniques of living on the plains were mastered.

A further set of changes in social structure is documented in Charles Callender's *Social Organization of the Central Algonkian Indians* (1962). He is primarily concerned with the tribes south of the Great Lakes, the Menomini, Potawatomi, Sauk, Fox, Kickapoo, Miami, Illinois, and Shawnee, who occupied the forest and prairie parklands of Illinois, Wisconsin, and Michigan. All these groups lived in semisedentary villages and practiced horticulture as well as hunting, and all were organized in terms of patrilineal clans or related groups, with dual divisions, and a "lineage" or Omaha type of kinship system. The social structure of these tribes parallels, in many respects, that of the Central Siouans of the Missouri region, whom we discussed in the last chapter, and their geographical contiguity has led Robert H. Lowie to explain the parallels in terms of diffusion.

But Callender sees the "Central Algonkian" social organization developing in this region in response to ecological, demographic, and cultural factors:

Abundant natural resources—such as wild rice—and the adoption of intensive agriculture brought about an expanded population, and an increase in the size of the bands, which became localized semi-permanent villages. Warfare and ritual activity probably forced consolidation into towns. These larger communities called for a large-scale social integration on a base broader than the kinship system alone [1962: 106].

Through the aid of Charles Hockett he was able to get some additional perspective on the kinship structures of both the southern and the northern Algonkian-speaking groups. Through comparison of cognate forms Hockett was able to reconstruct enough kinship terms to demonstrate the presence of cross-cousin marriage among proto–Central Algonkian populations. However, it was clear from the presence of alternate terms, that, while cross-cousin marriage was preferred, it was not completely specified.[2] As groups moved north and became differentiated

[2] Charles Hockett has recently published a revised version of "The Proto Central Algonquian Kinship System" (1964), in which he presents his reconstruction of PCA kinship terms. From these he infers (1) cross-cousin marriage of the stricter type (man with mother's brother's daughter) and (2) patrilocality.

He notes that "the relatedness of cousin, uncle-and-aunt, and nephew-and-niece terms to in-law terms is clear enough evidence for cross-cousin marriage of some sort" (1964: 765). The inference of matrilateral cross-cousin marriage and patrilocality is based on the suggestion that patrilocality would fit in with the usage of related terms for cross-aunt and mother-in-law, but of unrelated terms for cross-uncle and father-in-law.

This suggestion, if valid, will complicate the analysis here presented, since all the surviving cross-cousin marriage systems in the Northeast are bilateral rather than matrilateral. However, matrilateral cross-cousin marriage does occur among the Kaska, a northern Athabaskan tribe in Canada, according to Honigmann (1949).

as Cree, Naskapi, and northern Ojibwa, the cross-cousin marriage system became intensified and prescriptive. As portions of these groups moved onto the plains, the cross-cousin marriage systems shifted to wider-range generational systems, based on the importance of brothers. As groups moved south of the border, they gave up cross-cousin marriage in favor of "lineage" organized systems. Callender attributes this loss to such factors as larger populations incident to agriculture but also to the development of clan groups with more "corporate" functions and to a complex village organization. The clans, in particular, controlled supernatural power in the form of an eponym and stocks of names, with associated ritual functions organized around clan bundles. With population losses and disintegration the clan groups in some tribes such as the Fox and Shawnee, were transformed into "name" groups, no longer patrilineal lineages but social groups maintaining the bundle rituals for tribal welfare.

We can see part of this shift in Ruth Landes' as yet unpublished study of the Potawatomi, made in the 1930's. The Potawatomi, with the Ottawa, were closely related to the Ojibwa linguistically and formed one cultural group in pre-European times. In the early seventeenth century they resided in the region between Lake Michigan and Lake Huron, but Iroquois pressures and white incursions led to a complex series of movements in the eighteenth and nineteenth centuries, during which they broke up into several subgroups. The Prairie Potawatomi, who came to reside on a reservation in Kansas after forcible removal from the Illinois region in 1834–35, had a kinship system of the Omaha type, based on patrilineal lineages and clans, though many of the actual terms used were cognate with Ojibwa forms. Ruth Landes also secured some data on the Michigan Potawatomi from older informants who had resided there, which showed their system to be intermediate between the Ojibwa and Kansas Potawatomi. Thus the lineage organization of the mother's brother's descendants in the male line is not developed in the Michigan group, and the latter retains the Ojibwa term for "male cross-cousin," though not for "cross-cousin of the opposite sex." Marriage with the cross-cousin is not practiced, but there are sets of joking relationships reminiscent of the Ojibwa system. More recently, G. Quimby (1940) has shown that the Michigan group has shifted further toward the American white pattern..

Both Callender's and Landes' data support the assumption of a development of the Central Algonkian social systems from a cross-cousin model toward one based on a lineage organization, similar in many respects to that of the central Siouan groups. But, if Mathews' (1959) linguistic reconstruction of an original "Omaha" kinship pattern is correct for the Omaha and their relatives, it is clear that the two groups have developed their similarities in social structure in partial independence. Lowie's (1954: 94) explanation in terms of diffusion and borrowing holds only in part, and by looking beyond diffusion to the processes and factors of change we open up new and exciting vistas. Let me conclude this section of the argument by noting one or two further hypotheses.

We have seen that Rivers suggested the possibility that cross-cousin marriage formerly existed among some of the Dakota tribes, on the basis of Morgan's schedules. Somewhat later, Alexander Lesser made a comparative study of Siouan kinship terminologies for the purpose of further defining the Dakota, Omaha, and Crow types and for discovering possible functional relationships with other aspects of social structure. He found (1929, 1930) an empirical correlation of the Dakota type with a sibless band organization, of the Omaha type with patrilineal clans and of the Crow type with matrilineal clans. He sees the Dakota type as the basic form and as the direct result of the sororate and levirate, with Omaha and Crow types as later variations brought about by particular types of marriage, descent, and residence.

There is no evidence in the literature that the Dakota tribes ever practiced cross-cousin marriage, but in view of Morgan's data and the intermediate position of the Dakota between the Ojibwa and the Plains tribes I earlier suggested that "the Dakota kinship system was formerly based on cross-cousin marriage, but that under the influence of Plains life (and contacts) it was shifting to a 'Generation' type as exemplified by the Cheyenne" (1937: 95).

Since then, Hassrick has published his detailed account (1944) of the Teton Dakota kinship system, which shows that cross-cousins, while differentiated terminologically, behave as if they were "siblings," though less intensively. With regard to the terminology for cross-cousins, he says that there seems to have been a shifting of either terminology or the mode of behavior, since the terms are derived from the sibling-in-law terms plus the suffix -*si*, meaning "stop" or "go away." Hassrick thinks that there has been a shift in behavior patterns, since he finds no evidence of cross-cousin marriage or joking behavior between cross-cousins in recent times. But he finds (1944: 346–47) strong indications that "the Dakota have shifted the emphasis of their system from a lineal and collateral to an affinial organization," with "good terminological evidence of former cross-cousin marriage." He further suggests that "the entire shift may have been the result of a changing economy, for the system indicates an adjustment to the new Plains environment. The increased dependence upon the buffalo, and later the introduction of the horse demanded a dispersed mobility, and produced a larger population." On the modern reservation there is another change going on involving the breakdown of the old band organization and a greater emphasis on the conjugal family, and these changes, he says, are accompanied by "the return of cross-cousin marriage."

These tentative conclusions receive considerable confirmation at the other end of the Dakota series—among the Santee or eastern Dakota, who remained along the Mississippi River and in southern Minnesota while their linguistic and cultural relatives expanded onto the Plains. Later they participated in the great massacre of 1862, which led to their imprisonment and removal to the Santee reservation. Some were brought back to their old territory by missionaries, and from these and their descendants Ruth Landes has constructed a rather detailed account of their former social life, which is as yet unpublished.

The Santee resided in villages considerably larger than those of the Ojibwa. Each village was a kinship unit, for the most part, and closely identified with its land; trespass rules were kept. Each village was economically self-sufficient and hunted under the leadership of a shaman. Summer hunts for buffalo also occurred, sometimes in cooperation with other groups. The village was also the war-making unit; the village chief was normally a "peace chief," and a shaman was the war leader.

Each village was normally "exogamous," with marriage outside the range of kinship; residence was variable but probably patrilocal for chiefs, since chieftainship went

in the male line. Marriage required intervillage co-operation, as did games, which expressed intervillage rivalry
and usually ended in quarrels. There was one exception to
village solidarity of significance to the present problem—
the berdache was exiled from the village in a kindly but
mournful spirit.

The kinship system was a wide-range "classificatory"
system based on generation principles, differing from that
of the Ojibwa in not having most of the cross-cousin marriage equivalences and conforming to the Teton system
terminologically. But among the Santee the cross-cousin
relationship is a courting, flirting relationship in which
there is unmerciful teasing and hostility. Landes notes a
tendency to divert this courting relationship to siblings-in-
law, who are identified in behavior and use the same basic
linguistic terms. The Santee have forbidden the marriage
of relatives "throughout historical time," but they consider
the cross-cousin almost like a sibling-in-law, though cross-
cousins are counted as "siblings" so far as their children's
classification is concerned. Specifically, Landes says that
male cross-cousins joke and play sexually and can be
humiliated by one another in public without holding
offense. Female cross-cousins have a similar relationship,
but cross-sex cousins are more hostile and personal in
their relations. Siblings-in-law have parallel relationships,
but their behavior is bolder and, when of cross-sex, more
excited.

The exiling of the berdache from his native village is
intelligible in these contexts. His homosexual tendencies
made him act like a "cross-cousin" or "sister-in-law" to the
men of the village, and he was apparently expelled from
the village because of feelings that the village should be
exogamous. In the new village he is a stranger and can

have sex relations and even marry. He jokes with all, calling them "cross-cousins" or "siblings-in-law." In general he is the village clown and prostitute, and stories about the berdache deal with his sexual exploits.

Marriage was not allowed between relatives closer than fourth cousins, and it was felt to be wrong and dangerous for close relatives to marry. The proper form of marriage involved parental selection, with exchange of property between the family groups, but elopements resulted when the couple took matters into their own hands or were too closely related to marry in the regular fashion. Residence was often matrilocal, though there was no general rule. Women owned the houses, and there was a marked avoidance of the mother-in-law, though the avoidance might break down after a while if the son-in-law was a good provider. Mourning for a deceased spouse was violent, and remarriage was in terms of the sororate and levirate but without the controls exercised by the surviving spouse's clan as among the Ojibwa.

This interesting account gives us a picture of eastern Dakota social structure that is similar to Ojibwa in many ways but differs in village size and organization and in the important matter of cross-cousin marriage. If we assume that the Santee once had cross-cousin marriage but gave it up for various reasons, including increase in population density and village size and the necessity of co-operation for communal buffalo hunts and for protection against enemies, part of this picture becomes more intelligible. For, with the abandonment of cross-cousin marriage, the common status of "cross-cousin *and* sibling-in-law" is divided into two separate statuses. Since the joking and sexual behavior was still consonant with the "sibling-in-law" relationship, it apparently retained the old terms, whereas the "cross-cousin" relationship was no longer a marriageable one, and a suffix meaning "stop" or "go away" was apparently added as a temporary marker. Hence Landes found that, while both cross-cousins and siblings-in-law joked with one another, there was always tension involved, particularly with cross-cousins of the opposite sex, who thought in sexual terms but "had to repress part of it." There was considerable hostility expressed, sometimes in rape and sometimes in "eat-all" feasts of bear fat or muskrat fat. The stories of sexual and other exploits emphasized siblings-in-law more than cross-cousins, part of a tendency "to reduce the mating connotations to the vanishing point" for cross-cousins and to heighten the mating tendencies of siblings-in-law as expressed through the sororate and levirate.

But this state of affairs involves serious contradictions, which the Teton Dakota have apparently solved in behavioral terms. They maintain the same terminological patterns, but the behavior between cross-cousins approximates that of siblings, whereas the sibling-in-law behavior remains the same. The next stage in this process would apparently be to shift the terminology of cross-cousins to siblings, in keeping with the general Plains patterns, but the Teton Dakota were on the Plains for only three or four generations before being put on reservations. A test of this hypothesis can perhaps be made with the intermediate Dakota groups, the Yankton and Yanktonai, about whom we at present know relatively little.

This brief analysis suggests that in relatively well-controlled situations it may be possible to infer the former presence of an institution such as cross-cousin marriage with a considerable degree of probability, even in the absence of the institution in the ethnographic and historical records. In this connection I should emphasize that the foregoing interpretation is mine and not Ruth Landes— she nowhere in her paper suggests the possibility of former cross-cousin marriage among the Santee, and her evidence is all the more convincing for that very fact.

There is one further suggestion that may be presented that is particularly relevant to our understanding of the social systems of the Northeast. In the light of the parallels that Morgan noted between the kinship terminologies of the Dakota, Ojibwa, and Iroquois, it might be suggested, as a working hypothesis, that early Iroquois social structure was also based on cross-cousin marriage. Lafitau's description of Iroquois kinship indicates an Iroquois-Dakota type of terminology as early as 1724, and there is no latent evidence in the terms themselves for the marriage of cross-cousins. But there are hints in Iroquois culture relevant to such a marriage, and the earlier location of a portion of the Iroquois in the St. Lawrence region, under ecological conditions not too different from those of their northern Algonkian neighbors, may be significant. As these Iroquois moved, or were forced, south and west, the needs for stronger tribal organization may have been reflected first in the development of matrilineal moieties within the tribe and later in the development of the inter-tribal federation or league of the Iroquois. The traditional date for the latter is circa A.D. 1570 in the interim between Cartier's voyages and the first settlements in New France.

Moiety exogamy among the Iroquois might be a generalization, on a larger scale, of the intermarrying units involved in Ojibwa cross-cousin marriage, and the use of "sibling" terms for members of one's own generation and moiety and "cousin" terms for the members of the opposite moiety among the Iroquois would be consonant. Cross-cousin marriage has been explained in terms of moiety groupings ever since Tylor, but it is clear from the data we have been examining that the correlation is not very high. Why the Iroquois, with their relatively strong matrilineal clan system, and their households based on matrilocal residence, never developed a lineage or Crow type of kinship organization is a problem that further ethnohistorical research may resolve. It may be that the strength of the moiety pattern is relevant: the Tlingit of the Northwest Coast and their neighbors also have matrilineal exogamous moieties associated with cross-cousin marriage, and here also there are only limited extensions of a lineage or Crow type of kinship.

v

We have come a considerable way from Morgan's recognition of a common kinship pattern between the Iroquois and their Algonkian and Dakota neighbors. The key to our analysis has come by following up Morgan's discovery that "cousins marry among the Cree." Morgan had come to consider the marriage of consanguinei as stringently prohibited "amongst the greater part of the American Indian natives" (1871: 164), so he probably considered the Cree situation as evidence of cultural disintegration. Hence the evidence in Morgan's own tables as to partial equivalence of consanguineal and affinal terminologies for certain of these groups was never brought to the attention of anthropologists until Rivers made his suggestions over forty years later.

Hallowell was the first modern anthropologist to see the significance of cross-cousin marriage in the Northeast, and we have found his working hypothesis that "northern Algonkian kinship systems are . . . intelligible as variants of a basic pattern that has undergone modification as a result of acculturative processes and differences in local conditions" to be borne out by the results of later field research. We have paid considerable attention to ecological factors that are relevant to both the size and the organization of social groupings and have noted that changes in technological processes may bring about changes in the population ceiling, which, in turn, initiate changes in the social structure that may have far-reaching effects.

We have also made considerable use of historical controls, both by comparing variant systems of a common linguistic group and by utilizing the results of linguistic reconstruction and ethnohistorical research. These historical data not only add a new dimension to structural-functional analysis but also are important in determining the directions in which change has taken place. Charles Hockett's reconstructions of proto–Central Algonkian kinship terms, for example, make it possible to see the directions of change more accurately than can be done by comparison alone.

In the case of the Northeast, we have seen again that kinship terminologies are sensitive indicators of change, but we have also noted the significance of the behavior component in bringing about terminological modification. We have also suggested that cross-cousin marriage is not merely a "cultural trait" but represents a systematic way of solving certain problems that small-scale groups face in difficult environments when technological developments are at a low level.

For the Central Algonkians west and south of the Great Lakes, Callender's (1962: 74–79) hypothesis for the development of their social organization provides an explanation that takes account of ecological factors and the effects of agriculture, ritual activity, and warfare in bringing about classical Central Algonkian social structure. It has the further advantage of making the modern variant patterns intelligible in terms of acculturation, depopulation, and other factors. With regard to kinship patterns he finds:

> Central Algonkian kinship systems are moving from an Omaha structure into a generational and more completely bilateral system quite similar to the American pattern. Among conservative societies and in the older age levels the system still conforms to a lineage pattern, but its effective range has narrowed to exclude all but actual relatives except in such practices as ceremonial adoption which remains an important extension of kinship. The shift is much more pronounced among younger persons and in less conservative groups [1962: 101].

Kinship behavior passes through a parallel series of steps. In the bilateral and generational organization, cross and parallel lines are still distinguished, but all cross-cousins become mild joking relatives, which Callender thinks may be related to the partial return to marriage with second or third cross-cousins among some of the groups. The final stage is a system not much different from that of the surrounding whites.

The changes in clan organization are more complex, involving loss of kinship extension and exogamic functions. "Today," Callender says, "Central Algonkian clans are name groups to which other functions may be attached (1962: 102).

These changes under modern acculturation parallel in a general way those we have outlined above for the matrilineal groups of the Southeast and of the Missouri Valley. In both situations there was a shift from a lineage organization to a generational one, so far as kinship patterns were concerned, as well as a breakdown of the clan system. It is probable that both processes of change that we have outlined, the slow gradual shift found by Spoehr in the Southeast and the more rapid changes noted by Bruner for the Mandan-Hidatsa, are operative. We might expect patrilineal institutions to survive longer, since there is some patrilineal bias in white social organization.

With regard to the Dakota tribes, their movement out into the High Plains brought about changes that are related to those in the previous chapter. Here Morgan's suggestion that "a change in the mode of life among the Dakotas occurred . . . when they were forced upon the plains and fell into nomadic bands" (1877: 157–89) contains the basis for the hypothesis, which we have found useful.

The problem of clans among the Dakota is a puzzling one, in need of further ethnohistorical and comparative research. Morgan states in *Systems* that "when first known to the colonists, through the early explorers, they were subdivided into a number of independent bands, living more or less in tent villages" (1871: 171, quoting Carver 1796: 51). But later, in *Ancient Society* (1877: 158) he suggests that the Dakota once had a patrilineal clan organization, but had allowed it to decay. He notes that Carver, who was among the Dakota in 1767, remarks:

Every separate body of Indians is divided into bands or tribes; which band or tribe forms a little community within the nation to which it belongs. As the nation has some particular symbol by which it is distinguished from others, so each tribe has a badge from which it is denominated; as that of the eagle, the panther, the tiger, the buffalo, etc. . . . Throughout each nation they particularize themselves in the same manner, and the meanest person among them will remember his lineal descent and distinguish himself by his respective family [1796: 164].

Morgan goes on to state that when he visited the eastern and western Dakota in 1861–62 he could find no satisfactory traces of clans among them and suggests that "a change in the mode of life among the Dakotas occurred between these dates when they were forced upon the plains and fell into nomadic bands, which may, perhaps, explain the decadence of gentilism among them" (1877: 158–59).

Modern ethnographers have variant answers. Lesser found no clans among the Dakota in his field researches in the late 1920's, but Lowie says that the eastern branches of the Dakota "probably had patrilineal reckoning" (1954: 95), basing his statements on Carver and on Wissler's unpublished field notes for the Yankton and Yanktonai (personal communication). Ruth Landes likewise found no clans among the eastern Dakota in her 1935–36 field research, but her account, which should be published soon, clarifies some of the conflicts.

In a reassessment of the cultural position of the Dakota groups James Howard states: "All the Santee bands were divided into exogamous patrilineal clans . . . which were usually named after localities rather than animals, birds or other natural phenomena" (1960: 252). And, as with the southern Siouans, "each Santee clan had a specified place in the ceremonial camping circle, which was formed on the tribal bison hunt and for certain ceremonies." Howard further believes that clans were once present among the Yankton, Yanktonai, and Teton divisions but had disintegrated by the time scientific investigations took place.

The problem of the relations of totemic animals to social and ritual groups, and to individuals as guardian spirit protectors, is a complex one in this region, and both family and village units may be involved, as well as possibly descent groups. The eastern Dakota village apparently formed a semi-independent "corporate" group and utilized marriage and other types of alliance to maintain connections in the face of an expanding population. Here a detailed comparison with the Ojibwa expansion will be rewarding.

In his formulation of the stages of social evolution, Morgan laid much stress on his view that the American Indian, organized on the basis of communal clans, lacked any idea of private property, a conception that he believed underlay the European family and kinship terminology. If he had been able to investigate the "family hunting territories" of the northeastern Algonkian tribes he would have been forced to modify certain of his conclusions as to the basis for the "descriptive" systems of kinship terminology. How he would have handled the discovery of preferential cross-cousin marriage among these groups is not clear. In his larger evolutionary system, which he related to marriage patterns, cross-cousin marriage would have been considered as somewhere between the marriage of brothers and sisters and the American Indian system based on clan exogamy. As such it could have been fitted in, but in the process Morgan might well have taken a closer look at the relations that exist between terminology and forms of preferential marriage in more limited time periods. But once the larger picture came into focus Morgan came to worry less about such apparently minor variations in detail.

V

THE PUEBLO INDIANS IN MODERN
PERSPECTIVE:
UNITY IN DIVERSITY[1]

I

YOU WILL RECALL THAT LEWIS H. MORGAN HAD REACHED
the foot of the Rocky Mountains on his last field trip in
1862, after a journey of some two thousand miles up the
Missouri River by boat. Beyond the mountains, in western
North America, was to be found an Indian world of much
greater variety and complexity than Morgan ever realized,
since he had only fragmentary accounts from travelers
and missionaries for this whole region. A. L. Kroeber, in
his *Cultural and Natural Areas of Native North America*
(1939), allots three of his major culture types to this
region: the Northwest Coast, the Intermontane, and the

[1]For the discussion in this chapter I have relied heavily on my
Social Organization of the Western Pueblos (1950) and Edward P.
Dozier's various publications on the eastern Pueblos and Hopi-Tewa.
Edward H. Spicer's *Cycles of Conquest* (1962) presents the historical
background in excellent fashion, and I have profited greatly from the
papers in the special issue on "The Southwest" edited by Emil Haury
for the *American Anthropologist* and the discussion of the American
Southwest in *Seminars in Archaeology: 1955*, edited by Robert Wauchope *et al.* In addition, I have utilized discussions with John Connelly
and Alfonso Ortiz, students with special competence on the Hopi and
eastern Tewa, respectively.

Southwest, in addition to the Eskimo in the north and Mexico and Central America in the south, in contrast to the single culture type of the East and North with which we have so far been concerned. Morgan (1869) looked to the Columbia River region, with its rich resources in salmon, as a possible place for the expansion of Indian population and its subsequent dissemination throughout eastern North America, and he eagerly questioned Father DeSmet, the well-known Oregon missionary whom he found on board the "Spread Eagle," with regard to food resources and related matters.

The Pueblo Indians of the Southwest have been known since Coronado's expedition in 1540–42, and they have managed to preserve a portion of their lands and much of their way of life down to the present day. They reside in the semiarid Colorado plateau of northern Arizona and New Mexico, surrounded by the ruins of their ancestral villages, and cultivate native corn, beans, and squash, as well as peaches and other crops introduced by the Spaniards. They are the first Indians, of all we have surveyed, to live primarily by agriculture and to have permanent communities of adobe or sandstone houses. The men are the agriculturalists, and the women are responsible for the household and its activities and are—or were—the pottery makers.

Pueblo culture is both highly distinctive and uniform in its externals. From the Hopi in the west to Taos in the east the patterns of living are similar. And Ruth Benedict, in her famous *Patterns of Culture* (1934), described a distinctive ethos or world view, as well. The basic values of the Pueblos are Apollonian, she says, in contrast to the Dionysian pursuit of excess that characterizes other American Indians. "The Zuni are a ceremonious people, a people who value sobriety and inoffensiveness above all other virtues. Their cult of the masked gods, of healing, of the sun, of the sacred fetishes, of war, of the dead, are formal and established bodies of ritual with priestly officials and calendric observances" (1934: 59–60).

These basic and detailed similarities suggest that Pueblo culture has had a long and homogeneous history behind it. Yet, if we examine Pueblo social structure, we find major variations that are in sharp contrast to the cultural and psychological unity that is so clearly apparent. Thus the western Pueblos—Hopi, Hano, Zuni, Acoma, and Laguna—conform to a general pattern based on matrilineal exogamous clans, extended matrilocal households, and a "Crow" or lineage type of kinship system, whereas the eastern Pueblos of the Rio Grande region, particularly the Tewa villages, are primarily bilateral in social structure, with a dual division of the society associated with summer and winter, and a kinship system of "Eskimo" type in which seniority, or relative age, is emphasized. Political organization is diffuse and limited in the west but concentrated and strong in the east. The ceremonial societies are primarily concerned with rain in the west and with curing of illness in the east, though community welfare and fertility are important everywhere. Taking the Pueblos as a whole, there is gradual variation from west to east in these respects, rather than sharp breaks, but the extremes are radically different.

There are also important linguistic differences among the Pueblos, that cut across this division of social structure. Thus the Hopi Indians, whose nearest linguistic relations are with the Shoshonean groups in the Great Basin, are distantly related to the Tewa and other Tanoan-speakers in the Rio Grande, and Hano represents a Tewa-speaking group that fled to the Hopi region after the Pueblo Rebellion of 1680 and continued to reside with the Hopi on First Mesa. But Zuni seems to be a separate language group, with no close linguistic affiliations elsewhere, though Stanley Newman (1964) finds evidence for a distant relationship with California Penutian, and the Keresan-speaking pueblos in the central region likewise have no close linguistic kin. On the other hand, the Tanoans of the Rio Grande are subdivided into three dialect groups: the Tewa, Towa, and Tiwa, which are relatively close to one another. Their nearest relatives elsewhere are the Kiowa of the Plains.

The Southwest is also complex in another way, in that different culture types are found in the same general region with different ecological adaptations and different histories. Interspersed through the Pueblo region are various Navaho and Apache groups, Athabaskan-speaking peoples who broke off from their Canadian relatives in the north and made their way into the Plains and the Southwest some time before the Spaniards arrived. Farther south are the Pima and Papago, who speak languages distantly related to the Hopi and Basin Shoshoneans and to the Aztecs and other peoples in northern Mexico as well. In the lower Colorado River region Yuman-speaking tribes, such as the Mohave, Cocopa, Yuma, and Maricopa, developed a distinctive flood-plain agriculture, while their linguistic relatives, the Walapai, Yavapai, and Havasupai, were primarily hunters and food-gatherers on the neighboring plateaus.

Little of this complexity was known when Morgan finally visited the Southwest in 1878. On his first trip to Kansas in 1859 he had met a group of Taos traders who had come over the Santa Fe trail to Kansas City. Among them were a few Taos Indians, and he made arrangements to talk with them—but then, as now, they did not show up for the appointment. He did secure fragmentary schedules from Tesuque, a Tewa pueblo near Santa Fe, and Laguna, a Keresan village, from an Indian agent and missionary, respectively, but they were not complete enough for analysis. Twenty years later, when he took his grandnephews on a tour of southwestern Colorado and New Mexico, he spent most of his time surveying archeological sites in the San Juan and Mesa Verde regions. When he finally reached Taos, he was kindly received by the governor and taken into a kiva, a signal honor, but was somewhat disappointed in the size of Taos after seeing the great Aztec ruin in the San Juan region. But, when the Indians began to sing and dance in the evening, his enthusiasm returned: "They are Iroquois all over," he reports in his journal.

Morgan's pioneer observations on the San Juan ruins were made soon after they were brought to scientific attention, and he came to the conclusion that the San Juan region might possibly be the native region for the domestication of corn and an important center for the dissemination of agriculture. At the request of the newly organized Archaeological Institute of America, he outlined a plan for research and exploration in New Mexico, Arizona, and Central America, which led to the appointment of his friend Adolph F. Bandelier to undertake this task. Morgan thus was, in a real sense, the initiator of much of the early archeological and ethnological research in the Southwest, though he did not live to see the results.

II

American archeologists, led by A. V. Kidder, early concentrated their attention on the Pueblo Southwest, and
particularly on the San Juan region, and by 1927 had
established a series of stages of development from Basket-
maker beginnings to the modern pueblos. With the perfec-
tion of tree-ring dating by A. E. Douglass, these stages,
based on stratigraphy and pottery correspondences, could
be accurately dated, and all that seemed to remain was
to fit in the marginal sites. But the excavations in west-
central New Mexico and southern Arizona resulted in the
delineation of two new archeological cultures, the Mogol-
lon and the Hohokam, which had affiliations to the south
and seemed even older than the Pueblo culture to the
north. Archeologists are still working out the interrela-
tionships of these three puebloid traditions, but it seems
clear that their fusion in the thirteenth and fourteenth
centuries in the Little Colorado region gave rise to the
modern western Pueblos.

The abandonment of the San Juan–Mesa Verde region
during the thirteenth century, coincident with the growing desiccation that culminated in the great drought of
A.D. 1276–99, resulted in a wholesale movement of population to the Rio Grande, which had been only sparsely
populated in earlier centuries. Recent excavations in this
latter region (Ellis and Brody 1964) are beginning to
relate the Tewa, Tiwa, and Towa pueblos to particular
archeological regions on the basis of pottery types. Thus
the Tiwa ancestors of Taos Pueblo began to move into

the Rio Grande in small groups from the Piedra district of southern Colorado about A.D. 1100–1200, and the Tewa groups started moving from the Mesa Verde–McElmo region about A.D. 1200, though the major movements were apparently just before A.D. 1300. This is precisely the region in which Morgan made his archeological surveys and which he considered a major center for the dispersion of agriculture in the Southwest. Farther south in the Rio Grande region the early affiliations of the Towa pueblos are still obscure, but there is evidence in the Galisteo Basin south of Santa Fe of the intrusion of Keres or other ancestral populations about A.D. 1350. Farther to the west, in southern Arizona, Emil Haury (1950) has presented evidence to indicate that the modern Pima and Papago may be the descendants of the Hohokam peoples, who had extensive irrigation projects in the Salt and Gila River Valleys but who "disappeared" as archeological cultures about A.D. 1300. And in the lower Colorado River region and adjoining plateaus, the Patayan is probably ancestral to the modern Yuman-speaking populations.

These archeological findings indicate a far more complex history for the Southwest than was thought possible in 1930 and suggest some of the reasons for the variations we have noted in modern Pueblo culture, About A.D. 1300 there was a withdrawal of Pueblo populations from southern Utah and a fusion of the groups in the Little Colorado River region to give the cultural base for the modern Hopi pueblos and the Zuni villages. The Keresan pueblos apparently developed in the Mount Taylor region from the amalgamation of groups from farther north, and from this region and possibly also from the upper Little Colorado region there were movements into the nearby Rio Grande.

In the past decade archeologists have provided broader and deeper perspectives that are relevant to the common and continuing features of Pueblo life that have been mentioned. Recent excavations in the Great Basin and Intermontane regions have delineated a Desert Culture that has deep roots, a wide extension, and many ecological variants and that has a base different from that of the early hunting cultures of the Plains and the eastern regions. This food-gathering culture survived until modern times in the deserts of the Great Basin, but in marginal regions more favorable conditions led to the development of agriculture from wild-seed gathering and to a settled village life.

In the excavations of Jesse Jennings at Danger Cave (1957) in western Utah, we can see the Great Basin, at the end of the Pleistocene, some ten thousand years ago, gradually becoming warmer and dryer. As the Pleistocene lakes disappeared, so did the larger mammals, and the population that remained gradually shifted from the hunting of large game to the exploitation of other food resources. Wild seeds and piñon nuts became central to subsistence, and techniques for grinding seeds and other foods were developed that continue directly into the modern pueblos. Seasonal population shifts from valley floors to higher levels led to a limited nomadism, with small groups returning to sheltered spots for the winter season. With variations, this type of life was found over the whole Intermontane region, from British Columbia to southern Mexico. Out of it came basic anxieties about food, an intensive knowledge of and concern with nature, and a peaceful ethos that has characterized Pueblo life.

The recent discoveries in the Tehuacán valley in

southern Mexico by Richard MacNeish (1964) have out-lined the sequences by which food-gathering changed to food production, with the gradual domestication of various wild plants, including squash, beans, maize, and, later, cotton, beginning about 5000 B.C. Out of this develop-ment came ultimately the high civilizations of Mexico and Central America, and from these and related centers vari-ous aspects of the agricultural complex slowly diffused northward, reaching the cultures of the Southwest about 1000 B.C., or possibly earlier. Agriculture was only a sup-plement to food-gathering and the hunting of small game for many centuries, until it gradually assumed central im-portance in a few favorable regions. In these latter the small, seminomadic microbands began to build pit-house villages or to live in nearby caves, later to aggregate in larger surface communities. As irrigation was perfected, large-scale occupation of desert regions was possible, where water flow and topography were favorable.

Once Pueblo culture had mastered agricultural tech-niques, the population ceiling was raised and small com-munities expanded as far north as Great Salt Lake in Utah, only to retract as a result of growing drought and the possible incursions of Utes and early Athabaskans. This period was one of readjustment and extensive migra-tion, as we have seen. But by A.D. 1300, or soon after, the basis for the modern Pueblos was being established.

The advent of the Spaniards brought further major influences to bear on the Pueblos. Coronado's expedition in 1540–42 brought military defeat to Zuni and other villages and resulted in the requisitioning of both food and labor on a large scale. After Oñate established the first Spanish colony in the Rio Grande region in 1598, the Pueblos were systematically "reduced," and missions were established. So galling was the Spanish yoke that in 1680 the Pueblos united to drive the Spaniards out of New Mexico and held them at bay for twelve years. On their return the Spaniards exacted submission from all the Pueblos but left the Hopi villages largely to their own devices. In the Rio Grande region, however, Spanish acculturation was strong (Dozier 1961) and was met with passive resistance behind a wall of religious secrecy that is still in force today.

During the Spanish period various Athabaskan and Shoshonean groups rose to prominence as raiders, mainly through the acquisition of the horse. The Navaho, who had previously developed small-scale agriculture from contact with the eastern Pueblos, took over sheep and horses from the Spaniards and became primarily pastoralists who raided both the Spanish settlements and the Indian Pueblos in the intervals between truces and trading. In turn, the Navaho were gradually forced out of their homeland in northern New Mexico by Ute pressures and by Spanish expansion westward. The Comanche with newly acquired horses, arrived in the Staked Plains soon after A.D. 1700 and gradually took over much of the southern plains from Apache and other groups and, by 1838, had forced the abandonment of Pecos Pueblo on the eastern frontier.

With the independence of Mexico from Spain in 1821–22, the New Mexican colonies were largely left to defend themselves against Navaho, Apache, and Comanche raids, and trading relations were increasingly with the American settlements by way of the Santa Fe trail. New Mexico came into the possession of the United States after the Mexican War of 1846, and the army was given the task of restoring order on the new frontier. But not until Kit

Carson rounded up the Navaho in 1863–64, with the help of Hopi and other Pueblos, and Generals Miles and Crook captured Geronimo and his Apaches in 1886 was order restored. The administration of Indian affairs was long in the hands of the army, and schools and missions were not established until the latter part of the nineteenth century. Even after Arizona and New Mexico became states, progress was slow, and only since World War II have the Navaho and some of the Pueblos come into close contact with the modern world. Since then, the Navaho in particular have made rapid progress, owing largely to extensive royalties from natural gas and oil.

III

This brief survey of southwestern archeology and history suggests some of the complexities that we need to control if we are to understand the modern Pueblo peoples and their neighbors. There are many fascinating problems to pursue, but we might now return to the differences we have briefly noted between the social structures of the eastern and western Pueblos and see to what extent we can account for them.

The western Pueblos—Hopi, Hano, Zuni, Acoma, and Laguna—all live in a semidesert environment, where rainfall is uncertain and arable land is limited. All conceive of their societies as in a "steady state," unfolding according to a preordained pattern and continuing in a "timeless" existence. All are organized in terms of matrilineal descent and matrilocal residence, with kinship systems of Crow or lineage type, as we have already seen.

Since the Hopi preserve more of their aboriginal character than the other western Pueblos, we might examine them in more detail. The Hopi have resided in a number of villages on the southern edge of Black Mesa for well over one thousand years. Their ancestors were undoubtedly attracted to this region by the small springs that flow from the margins of the mesas, and we find them living in small communities as early as A.D. 500–700. Despite an agricultural technology, limited rainfall and floodwater farming have restricted the size of villages and the total population to around 2,500 until modern times. The villages are distributed on three mesas, with about 800–900 persons on each.

Time after time during their long history the Hopi have faced the threat of extinction or dispersal through periodic drought or epidemic disease. During the latter half of their history nomadic enemies entered the region, and later, in 1629, the Spaniards established missions for a fifty-year period. With the Pueblo Rebellion of 1680, the Tewa and other refugees fled to the Hopi country, some remaining to become the Hopi-Tewa of the village of Hano.

During that period the Hopi never created a political community, or developed the use of force to any great extent. Rather, they relied on dispersal of their villages, constructed in part for defense, and on a reputation for superior supernatural assistance, to ward off their enemies. Within their small communities they developed an elaborate clan system, to which was attached the most valuable agricultural lands, and the control of ceremonies and deities. The ceremonial cycle was conducted by societies that cut across the clan system but were tied to individual clans. The Hopi way, embodied in myth and tradition, was maintained by an elaborate system of training and indoctrination, culminating in a series of initiation rituals, and by the important sanctions of public opinion. Crises involving the possibilities of major change were handled through the development of factions, which might lead to village-splitting and the establishment of new communities.

The Hopi model for their society centers on a traditional "mother" village, a "colony" village, and a "guard" or protector village, and this pattern is repeated on most of the mesas. On Third Mesa, Oraibi had reached an unmanageable size by the 1890's and had already established a colony at Moencopi. In 1906, Oraibi split in two, and half the population who wished to maintain the Hopi way of life without governmental interference, moved away to found the conservative village of Hotevilla.

Each major Hopi village is an independent unit and tends toward endogamy, except for intermarriage with colony villages. On First Mesa the Tewa have maintained their social identity and language, in the face of growing intermarriage with the Hopi, by a strict observance of matrilocal residence. In Hopi theory each major village is composed of matrilineal clans whose position in the village is determined by the order of arrival and the ceremonial possessions they brought with them. Each major clan has a named clan house in the village in which the ceremonial possessions are kept, and associated with the clan house are the clan lands traditionally assigned to the clan and from which it gets its major support. At the head of the prestige hierarchy is the Bear Clan, the members of which arrived first in the Hopi region and made a compact with Masau'u, the god of life and death, in which he gave the Hopi lands and crops in exchange for carrying out the proper rituals. Later-comers received portions of this estate in exchange for the performance of ceremonies for rain for the crops, but the "last" arrivals often possessed no rituals and offered their services as guards. Their position was marginal, and usually they were not assigned clan lands.

Within the village we can see that the clan is often divided into one or more lineages. One lineage, or lineage segment, occupies the clan house and looks after the ritual possessions of the clan, while other lineages support the "prime" lineage in carrying out its duties. Lineage extinction is common at this level, and supporting lineages are prepared to move into the clan house on such occasions. When a whole clan becomes extinct, a related clan from the same phratry may move into the clan house and gradually assume its name and position. Conversely, marginal lineages are expendable in times of crisis. In case of drought, all resources are concentrated for the preservation of the central clan core, and other clansmen may be forced to migrate or starve. As conditions improve, they may return and take up their former position and activities.

The Hopi household is composed of a line of women who look to their husbands for economic support and to their brothers for ritual support. Marriage is monogamous and men circulate in Hopi society. They join their wives' households, first as husbands and later as fathers. Here they have few rights, to begin with, and ideally play a passive role, giving advice when asked but not interfering in household and lineage matters. They retain their ties to their natal households, however, where they are responsible for the discipline of their sister's sons and the proper performance of ritual roles. The tension between these contrasting roles is one of the reasons for the high divorce rate among the Hopi.

Marriage is arranged primarily by the individuals concerned, but the first marriage involves special ceremonies and a reciprocal exchange of food and clothing between the two households. Men married into a household cooperate for its support, but the crops raised belong to the women of the household. Men also herd sheep for both wool and meat, since their introduction in Spanish times, but sheep have acquired little ritual value. Married women are expected to aid their husband's sisters and clanswomen on ritual occasions, helping with corn-grinding, cooking, and piki-making. The household is of more enduring importance to women, and the houses belong to them. Without a household to support him a man cannot carry out his ceremonial duties properly in Hopi society.

Men find their major interests and activities in the ceremonial system. A "ceremonial father" inducts a boy into the Katcina cult and later into one of the four men's societies involved in the tribal initiation ceremonies, as well as into any other societies he happens to belong to. Since the "ceremonial father" is normally not a relative, the membership of these societies cuts across clan lines and represents a cross-section of the total society. Each ceremony is "owned" by a particular clan which furnishes the chief priest and maintains the altars. Hence an individual's potential status is established more or less at birth. Marriage into key households and induction into the proper kivas, however, offer possibilities of achieving a higher ceremonial position.

Community welfare has a high social value, and cooperation rather than competition is stressed in Hopi society. Individuals are not supposed to aspire to higher status positions within the ceremonial system. But competition between household groups and between kiva groups is strong. Clans move up in status by taking over vacated positions and gradually making them their own. And there is a further competition between villages involving both ceremonial performance and hospitality.

Hopi society achieves and maintains continuity both through the clan-phratry system and the fiction that a clan never "dies" and through the continued performance of ceremonies in calendric sequence. In Hopi theory the souls of the living come from the underworld, to which the dead return. But the ancestors have a continuing responsibility to their descendants, and as katcina and cloud they return periodically to provide both gifts for the children and rain for the crops.

Hopi society meets recurring crises, both by maintaining a surplus of food for lean years and by sloughing off the less "valuable" members of various clans and lineage groups. The role of the village chief in these crises is a passive one; he is a "father" rather than an "uncle" and is ideally detached but sympathetic and deeply interested and concerned with the welfare of all his "children." But the theocratic organization of the Hopi frequently has to struggle with political problems, particularly in modern times. These problems are generally dealt with by factions that explore alternatives in terms of traditional teaching and the realities of the situation. In the American period these factions have not always been kept within bounds, and on Third Mesa the split that began with the founding of Hotevilla in 1906 has now resulted in six separate communities.

The other western Pueblos have developed somewhat differently from a common sociocultural base, as I have elsewhere noted (1950). Thus Zuni, originally composed of some six villages at the time of the Pueblo Rebellion in 1680, united into a single community thereafter and developed a central religious hierarchy and centralized political power to maintain discipline and unity in the face of the Spanish threat. But Zuni had sufficient water for Pueblo needs, and summer farming villages grew up in favorable localities. At Acoma a disastrous defeat by the Spaniards resulted in a similar centralization of power in the hands of a single clan. Here permanent farming villages were also established away from the mother village. Laguna has had a somewhat different history, in which strong missionary influence and leadership led to the migration of conservatives to Isleta in the nineteenth century, with the resulting breakdown of the Laguna ceremonial system and the dispersal of the population in farming villages.

In all these communities there is a close correlation of descent, residence, and kinship. Women are central to the clan and household, while men divide their time between economic activities and ritual performance. As one goes eastward, curing rituals and the medicine societies become more important, though the katcina cult is still strong. With the eastern Keresans new elements begin to enter from the Rio Grande region, which bring about further changes.

IV

The eastern Pueblos of the Rio Grande region are divided, as we have seen, into a number of language groups. In the north the Tiwa-speaking villages of Taos and Picuris are separated from their close linguistic relatives at Isleta and Sandia in the Albuquerque region. The Towa are today limited to the pueblo of Jemez on a western tributary of the Rio Grande but formerly also occupied Pecos Pueblo, on the edge of the Plains. In the center are the five Tewa-speaking pueblos, San Juan, Santa Clara, San Ildefonso, Nambé, and Tesuque, who occupy the Rio Grande valley north of Santa Fe. The eastern Keres villages are separated from their close western relatives and occupy the Rio Grande and adjacent streams south of Santa Fe.

None of the eastern Pueblos is adequately known as yet. As the Spaniards attempted to stamp out the katcina dances and pagan ceremonies, the villagers conformed outwardly and became nominal Catholics but continued to maintain their own religion in secret. But we do have an outline of Tewa social organization and enough information to sketch the more important similarities and differences.

The environmental condition in the Rio Grande region is generally similar to that of the mesa country to the west, though the presence of mountain ranges gives somewhat greater variety. The most significant difference is undoubtedly the presence of the Rio Grande itself, which not only provided a constant supply of drinking water but also permitted irrigation. We shall see that the requirements of an expanded economy based on irrigation may be one important factor determining community organization.

The Tewa approximate the Hopi in total population and village size, with some 2,000 people in five villages ranging in size from 150 to 800 each. Each Tewa village is a political unit and is largely endogamous. There is no overall Tewa political organization, but there is some ceremonial cooperation among the Tewa villages as well as with other Rio Grande pueblos. The Tewa bore the brunt of Spanish pressures, both before and after the Pueblo Rebellion of 1680, and in modern times they have had to fight for their lands against the encroachment of neighbors and withstand internal dissension.

Each village is divided into two divisions or moieties (Ortiz 1965), associated with summer and winter, which alternate in control of the community approximately from equinox to equinox. These dual divisions are generally patrilineal but do not control marriage. Children are initiated into the moiety to which their father belongs, but changes of moiety affiliation are possible. Marriage tends to be within the moiety in some villages and a wife from the opposite moiety usually shifts to that of her husband.

Each moiety has a small group of officials composed of the cacique, or head priest, and his right- and left-hand assistants, plus a limited number of members who are recruited by dedication during illness or otherwise. The cacique and his assistants serve for life and move up in regular order. The moiety associations are responsible for the governmental and ceremonial activities of the community during their half of the year and for the selection and installation of the governor and his assistants, who represent the secular system imposed by the Spaniards in the seventeenth century to facilitate their program.

The summer and winter caciques and their assistants organize the ceremonies and dances, the cleaning and purification of the village, the hunt and war ceremonials, the construction and cleaning of the irrigation ditches, the repair of kivas and other communal property, and all planting and harvesting activities. All members of the community are required to obey the officials appointed to supervise these activities, under penalty of fines or other punishment, including expulsion from the community and confiscation of property.

Within the village are a number of other organizations that assist in various activities. The Katcina cult, in which ancestral spirits are portrayed by masked impersonators, is organized on moiety lines, all males automatically becoming members of the Katcina cult of their own moiety and, after puberty, participating in its rituals under the direction of a group of katcina officials. The katcina live underneath the mythical "lake of emergence" whence they are "brought" to the village by the two clown groups. The summer gods are brought from a lake to the south, the winter gods from the north. But other societies—the medicine or curing groups, the hunt group, the men's and women's war societies, and the clown groups—crosscut the moiety organization and thus aid in village integration. Membership in these associations is voluntary and is validated by initiation rituals following puberty. Each society holds monthly "retreats" and conducts its own ceremonies, as well as cooperating in the major ceremonies for the whole community. The clowns have the further responsibility of exposing wrongdoers to public ridicule and shame.

The Tewa thus have a small central group of officials who primarily perform ritual duties but who also wield great power. They control the allotment of pueblo lands for agriculture and house sites and can maintain discipline with the ultimate sanction of expulsion from the community. This central core, the "Completed People," as the Tewa call them, are responsible for maintaining traditional practices and continuity against the pressures for change. Surrounding them are the ordinary Tewa, the "Weed People," who are commoners and less valuable. And, living under the "lake of emergence" or in the mountains and elsewhere, are the ancestors and deities, who watch over the actions and hearts of their descendants.

The Tewa household, in contrast to its Hopi counterpart, is bilaterally organized and is primarily concerned with domestic functions. It usually consists of a set of grandparents, some of their children with their spouses, and the children of the latter. Normally, each nuclear family within the group has a set of separate but adjacent rooms, but the household cooperates closely in economic activities and the sharing of food and other resources. The household is an exogamic unit, and the members refer to one another as *matui*—"relatives"—and may also act as a unit in ritual matters. Residence is variable and depends on the availability of housing and land as well as on personality factors. Divorce or separation is rare; when it happens, one or the other spouse will return to his natal household, giving up all rights in his former spouse's household but often continuing relations with the children.

The Tewa kinship system is also quite different from that of the western Pueblos. It is bilateral and generational, with kinship terms being widely extended. The same terms are used for cross- and parallel cousins, as in our English system, but the terms themselves are derived from those used for parental younger siblings. Within the kinship system, seniority, or relative age, is highly important, and there is an extensive use of senior and junior reciprocals and a frequent absence of sex distinctions. While kinship terms are widely extended, the basic relationships are found in the household and center on the senior couple. Discipline is normally in the hands of the parents, but serious offenses may be taken to the moiety officials and punished by the war captains.

It is clear even from this brief summary that formal Tewa social structure is quite different from that which we have sketched for the Hopi. Here the community is central and is organized for community activities and community ends. There is little or no use of the principle of unilineal descent, except with regard to the broad membership in the dual divisions. While "clans" have been reported for the Tewa, they are either absent or, at best, vestigial. The ceremonial societies of the Hopi operate on a broad basis and through a process of recruitment that insures a representative cross-section, though control is vested in particular clans. The Tewa societies are smaller and more specialized and maintain continuity by a process of recruitment through dedication or by ceremonial "trapping" of new members. Only the Katcina cult is comparable in the two groups, but its operation in the Rio Grande region is diminished. As one Indian stated: "We have the Rio Grande for irrigation and don't have to dance for rain like the Hopis and Zunis."

The household in both regions has similar domestic functions, but the Hopi household is tied into the clan organization and has a continuity that the Tewa household lacks. The latter forms a unit in the moiety organization but has a greater flexibility in organization and little ceremonial responsibility. The sharpest contrast perhaps is with regard to the kinship systems: each is organized quite differently and the two contrast at almost every point.

V

One of the important tasks facing social anthropology is to explain both similarities and differences in social structures. Lewis H. Morgan, as we have seen, was primarily concerned with establishing the basic unity of American Indian social systems, and he tended to neglect differences in terms of what he thought was the overall unity. We have noted in previous chapters the progress in understanding and generalization that might be made by paying attention to differences, with particular reference to kinship systems. Here in the Southwest we face the problem of how to explain the basic differences in overall social structure between the eastern and the western Pueblos, in light of the fact that Pueblo culture conforms otherwise to a single cultural type.

Earlier explanations by E. C. Parsons and other Pueblo specialists, who first noted these differences, evoked diffusion from one or another Pueblo area to explain certain differences and differential Spanish acculturation as the reason for others. Thus the Katcina cult is strong in the west but diminishes in the east, with masked dancing entirely absent from Taos and Picuris. Medicine societies, on the other hand, are central in the Keresan pueblos but absent in Hopi and probably also in Taos. Dual divisions are strong in the Tewa pueblos and moderately developed in the eastern Keresan communities, but they occur only in symbolic form in the western Keresans and Zuni.

Similarly, the system of secular government in all the Pueblos except the Hopi, the use of Spanish as a lingua franca, and Catholic observances in the life cycle are obvious additions, as are the domestic animals and plants that the Spaniards introduced. But the family and kinship patterns are not the result of Spanish influence, despite some superficial resemblances, and the use of godparent relationships is without the significance attached to it by Catholics. Nor is witchcraft among the Pueblos an introduction by the Spanish despite European conceptions that have been incorporated into the complex of beliefs surrounding it.

If we are to understand the differences between the social structures of the eastern and the western Pueblos, we need to know, first, whether they derive from a common basic type or from different types. There is some economy in assuming a single earlier type, but we also need to keep alternative hypotheses in mind. Second, social structures have tasks to perform in maintaining social continuity and in meeting the needs of the community. For these purposes some structures are more efficient than others. Third, social structures change more often from internal readjustments than from external contacts. Borrowing may take place, but innovation and remodeling of existing structures are more common. And, last, we need to remember that different structures may perform similar functions.

Julian Steward (1937) has provided a model for the development of a clan system from band organization, which he has applied to the development of southwestern society generally and which I have found relevant to the Hopi sequence, as seen both archeologically and ethnologically. For the Hopi I have argued (1950) that they have developed out of a Great Basin type of social structure, through the localization of small groups around permanent sources of water and the gradual transition from seed-collecting to agricultural activities. The importance of women in these activities and the greater efficiency of cooperation in grinding and preparation led to matrilocal residence and matrilineal descent. The assumption by archeologists that the small communities of early Pueblo times were probably inhabited by matrilineal lineages can now be tested with fine-scale pottery analysis, as William Longacre has recently demonstrated (1964) for the Little Colorado region, and it is to be hoped that Douglas Osborne's current excavations in the Mesa Verde region will aid us in interpreting the early social organization of the Rio Grande region.

I have also argued that the Tewa probably had a social organization of the general western Pueblo type but that the conditions under which abandonment of the Mesa Verde and adjoining regions took place was not conducive to maintaining a complex social structure. Recent excavations in the Taos region (Ellis and Brody 1964) have shown that the populations ancestral to Taos filtered into the Rio Grande in small groups and were only gradually consolidated into larger communities, which may also have been true for the Tewa. Further, the adjustment to new conditions in the Rio Grande—including the development of irrigation projects—and the necessity for protection against nomadic invaders would require communal effort and central direction.

My own guess is that the dual organization began to develop soon after reaching the Rio Grande. The dual principle is the simplest form of segmentary organization and operates most effectively in relatively small groups.

The patrilineal tendencies may have developed in terms both of the increasing importance of men in agricultural activities and of the centralization of ceremonial and political activities. In any case the organization of major activities in terms of the moiety division and its symbolic association with summer and winter and of the associated natural phenomena suggests a long period of development.

G. P. Murdock, on the other hand, believes that the "Eastern Pueblo type of social structure is the earlier" (1951: 250) and prefers Florence Hawley's (1937) hypothesis that the western Pueblo subtypes later influenced the western Keresans and Jemez so that the latter acquired a western veneer. Hawley's hypothesis at that time assumed that the Tewa and related groups moved into the Southwest from the Plains, but she has since accepted their derivation from the Colorado region. Murdock further notes the striking lack of integration between kin groups and ceremonials among the Keresans, in contradistinction to the Hopi and Zuni. But in the western Keres villages, the matrilineal clans are corporate groups regulating the use and ownership of land, houses, and ceremonial property. In the east, as Dozier has noted (1960), these corporate functions are vested in the medicine societies, and the village chief comes from a particular medicine society, his clan affiliation being irrelevant. Since the medicine societies are voluntary associations, the result is a highly centralized political and ceremonial community. The kinship system also varies from west to east, and there is evidence that the shift is from a Crow or lineage type to a generation type, rather than the reverse. For these reasons I believe my original hypothesis continues to be useful, though still speculative.

Karl Wittfogel and Esther Goldfrank (1943) have

called attention to the importance of irrigation in the Southwest in relation to community cooperation and central direction, and Edward Dozier has supported them:

Irrigation and the tasks associated with it are the most important communal projects of the Rio Grande pueblos. One or two irrigation canals, running for several miles, are constructed from the headwaters of the main stream or streams, and engineered to bring just the proper amount of water. . . to the garden plots which surround each village. Near the village is a network of diverting ditches running off the main canals and into individual family land holdings. While the small irrigation ditches near the village are constructed and maintained by individual families, the larger canals must be constructed and periodically cleaned by the able-bodied members of the whole community under the supervision of officers whose positions are prescribed by the socio-political organization of each village. . . . Irrigation thus necessitates a socio-political organization which has a control over the community and one which may insure the proper functioning of the society with regard to its basic economy [1960: 150–51].

In addition, the necessities for defense, first against nomadic enemies and later to ward off the Spaniards and Americans, would intensify internal controls. Control over land and the threat of expulsion have served to maintain a united community in most villages, though veterans of World War II and the new opportunities for work at Los Alamos and in Santa Fe and Albuquerque are beginning to bring about modifications.

From these standpoints the shifts in social structure of the Keresan communities in the Rio Grande region represent parallel adjustments to the new requirements of life. Here, as we have seen, the medicine societies have a central role in selecting the village cacique, and there is a highly centralized political and ceremonial community.

The moiety pattern of the Tewa may have been borrowed, but it is here represented primarily in the dual ceremonial organization associated with the two large kivas that are characteristic of eastern Keresan communities, and it operates in a manner quite different from that among the Tewa.

The Tewa who moved from the Rio Grande after 1696 to escape Spanish vengeance and remained among the Hopi of First Mesa as the Hopi-Tewa of Hano show us the reverse situation. Here, in Dozier's excellent study (1954), we can see a refugee group making a place for themselves and maintaining their position by developing a mythology and an attitude of superiority, as well as by the strict observance of matrilocal residence. Today there are no pure-blooded Tewa, but socially they are still highly distinctive in language and, to a certain degree, in custom.

With regard to social structure, however, they have come to approximate the Hopi model. "Thus Hopi-Tewa social and ceremonial organization is founded on the same principles as the Hopi: the kinship system, household, clan, ceremonial societies, and kiva groups" are all similar. But Dozier notes (1954) that there are also similarities to the eastern Tewa in all these areas, and particularly in the ceremonial organization. Thus the Hopi-Tewa emphasize the moiety concept to a greater extent. There are two kiva groups at Hano, with separate ceremonies and a chief for each group, and the initiations "are suggestive of Tewa initiation rituals in New Mexico," The Katcina cult and the emphasis on curing rituals also indicate retention of Rio Grande patterns, in part at least.

Barbara Freire-Marreco, who studied both the Hano and Santa Clara Tewa more than forty years ago, assumed

(1914) that the Hano system was once common to both and that the eastern Tewa system had changed as a result of Spanish acculturation. But the "paternal clans" she found in the New Mexico Tewa villages are only vague "name groups" and may well have been borrowed from their Keresan neighbors to facilitate visiting or as imitations of Spanish patronyms. The retention of part of the Tewa moiety pattern and the rearrangement of kinship terms at Hano to fit a Crow pattern, without evidence of more than minor borrowing of actual terms, suggests that the Hopi-Tewa have shifted from an eastern Tewa moiety pattern, with bilateral kinship structure, to a matrilineal clan-phratry organization, and related kinship system, of the western Pueblo type.

Here we have a documented case of acculturation in which both participants are Indian tribes and in which no strong pressures for conforming to a radically different type of life are involved. As Dozier notes:

Hopi-Tewa social and ceremonial organization thus appear to be the result of (1) a core of elements indigenous to the group and bearing resemblances to the Rio Grande Tewa, (2) elements borrowed from the Hopi over a period of two and a half centuries during which the two groups lived as neighbors, and (3) a unique integration of the two that appears to be becoming progressively a new whole [1954: 368].

A further and quite unexpected result is the apparent development of a new personality type among the Hopi-Tewa. According to Dozier:

The Hopi-Tewa appears to be more aggressive, and more willing to accept white ways and to cooperate with the local Indian Service than his Hopi counterpart. The individual Hopi-Tewa is friendly to whites and has little of the reticence characteristic of both the Hopi and the Rio Grande Tewa [1954: 367].

Dozier ventures some suggestions as to the reasons for these contrasts, but they represent an interesting problem for further investigation. Here is a situation in which we may be able to investigate the relations of society, culture, and personality under relatively controlled conditions.

A region such as the Southwest is like an iceberg, in that what we see is only a small part of the whole. But anthropology is developing methods and techniques for unraveling past history and relationships, which will make much more of the past visible. In this brief discussion we have not "explained" the basic differences in social structure between the eastern and the western Pueblos, in any real sense, but we have gone beyond borrowing and diffusion to outline the framework within which such explanation should take place and have indicated some of the hypotheses that are currently under consideration. For the social anthropologist, the Southwest is just entering its most interesting period.

LEWIS H. MORGAN AND THE
FUTURE OF THE AMERICAN INDIAN[1]

I

LEWIS H. MORGAN WAS VITALLY INTERESTED IN THE FUTURE
of the American Indian, and—unlike many of his contemporaries—he believed the Indian had a future. Through
his pioneer researches on the Iroquois, Morgan was one
of the first scholars to see the problems of the Indians
from *their* point of view and to discuss the alternatives
to extinction. The problems facing the Iroquois seemed
fairly simple, but during Morgan's lifetime tremendous
changes took place as the frontier moved westward and
finally reached the Pacific, and at the time of his death
in 1881 the Indian question seemed further from solution
than ever.

Morgan's own ideas also changed. In his final discussion of the "Indian Question" (1878) he pointed out the
total failure of the present system with regard to the
400,000 Indians still remaining in the United States at
that date and laid down some guidelines for future policy:

They and their posterity will live in our midst for centuries
to come, because Indian arts for the maintenance of life are

[1] A briefer version under the same title, has been published (Eggan
1965).

142

far more persistent and effective than we are disposed to credit. The Indian tribes hold a more important position in relation to us than their numbers would imply. It is for this reason that they form no part of our social and political system, are not a part of our people, and stand without the pale of Government. But as the aborigines of the country and its ancient proprietors, they stand to us in a special relation—a relation in some respects awful to contemplate. We are responsible for them before mankind if we do not perform our duty towards them intelligently and as it becomes the superior race [1878: 332]:

As to what our duty toward the American Indian was, Morgan was quite clear. He had early expressed the view that the only hope for the Iroquois of New York State was in becoming agricultural and civilized, and ultimately citizens, with the same privileges and obligations as whites. These objectives, he believed, could be obtained through education and Christianity, and he saw the mission boarding school as the best instrument for the purpose. But the education and Christianization of the Iroquois was a subject of too much importance to be left to the limited means of religious societies, and he advocated either a system of public Indian education or the subsidization of the missions. "It is time," he said, "that our Indian youth were regarded, in all respects, as a part of the children of the State, and brought under such a system of tutelage as that relation would impose" (1851: 453).

But this turned out to be a more difficult transition for the nomadic Plains Indians recently settled on reservations on the western frontier, and here Morgan invoked the stages of cultural evolution that he had worked out in *Ancient Society*:

We wonder that our Indians cannot civilize; but how

could they, any more than our own remote barbarous ancestors, jump ethnical periods? They have the skulls and brains of barbarians, and must grow toward civilization as all mankind have done who attained to it by a progressive experience [1878: 332].

Hence he proposed that the Plains tribes be assisted in developing a "pastoral system" as an intermediate stage in their development toward civilization.

Today the "Indian problem" is still with us, in more complex fashion than ever before and with a wider relevancy for newly emerging nations in other parts of the world who also have minority groups. We still put our faith in education and good works, plus new techniques in agriculture and industry. But the work of Franz Boas and his students, plus the evidence before our eyes, is sufficient to convince most of us that the transition from "savagery" to the forms of "civilization" is not a function of race, nor does it have to pass through a regular series of stages. Since 1924 the American Indians have been citizens of the United States by Act of Congress, and thus have achieved one important goal, even though with regard to the individual states the citizenship is often "second class." But in most areas they still stand apart from the social and political life of the dominant whites, and their demands for justice and understanding still fall on uncomprehending ears.

It may well be that the Indian problem, in its present phrasing, is an insoluble one. In broad perspective there are only two solutions: (1) assimilation, either physically or culturally, or both, and (2) autonomy with equality. Long-term official policy has been oriented to the integration of Indian groups into American life, but the alternation of our political parties in office has resulted in a continual oscillation between these poles. For the American "melting pot" to operate effectively, there needs to be strong aspirations toward the new way of life and a willingness to give up old ties, loyalties, and values and replace them with new ones. For most immigrant groups this decision was a conscious and voluntary one, which was implemented at the expense of breaking up their old social and cultural life and integrating the fragments into the larger American whole. The transition was difficult for many, as our literature attests, and often required several generations to accomplish under the best of circumstances. In retrospect, the process is still far from complete.

The Indians were in a different position and have had a different experience. They had been defeated in war, deprived of their homelands, herded onto reservations that were inadequate to support them, and isolated from the main streams of activity, so the processes of assimilation had little opportunity to work. And, while Indian tribes were treated as "sovereign nations" in the making of treaties up until 1871, their actual status was that of wards, dependent on the government for subsistence and tutelage. American society, which can tolerate only limited variation from the majority norms, has periodically forced the Indian off the reservation by allotting the land and selling the surplus to whites or by luring him to the city with the promise of employment and a better life. But these periods have alternated with efforts to maintain and improve Indian life on the reservations by providing more adequate schools, better housing, improved agriculture, and modern health services. In the lifetime of many Indians, they have seen their lands allotted, their children taken off to boarding school, their ceremonies prohibited, and other changes forcibly prescribed. They have also been urged to reorganize their populations as tribal corporations, improve their reservation resources, develop new forms of political structure, and maintain their Indianness. Since World War II, John Collier's "new deal" for the Indians has given way, first to a policy of off-reservation migration, then to a policy of termination of federal control, and currently back to a policy of improving the resources for reservation living.

Faced with these rapid reversals of policy, individual Indians have either taken advantage of immediate opportunities or retreated into passive resistance. Of the 500,000 and more Indians now in the United States, some 60 per cent are still on reservations, and, with greater mobility and the development of the Pan Indian movement, the ties between reservation and non-reservation Indians are being strengthened.

As social anthropologists, we are primarily concerned with evaluating the alternatives in terms of the contact situation. We are beginning to see that Morgan's suggestion that "Indian arts for the maintenance of life are far more persistent and effective than we are disposed to credit" holds one key to the situation. As he earlier noted: "To form a judgment of the Indian character which is founded upon a knowledge of his motives and principles of action, he must be seen in his social relations" (1851: 305).

Tribal society and culture on the reservation, though often profoundly changed, are also very much alive. Here Morgan's emphasis on the importance of kinship and clan ties in Indian society, and the communal character of property and sharing, is relevant—and Indians living in the alien city frequently return to the reservation to renew these bonds. The role of the reservation as a "refuge" is partly psychological but also has deep social roots. And many reservation "home lands" have acquired a religious significance that goes beyond the present. There both the Indian and his ancestors are "at home."

An important factor in maintaining Indian identity is their growing opposition to white control, which sometimes takes the form of "revitalization" movements or nationalism, but more frequently takes the form of public appeals for justice and support, often in connection with political action. Opposition is a powerful influence for unity, and the minority Indians are being aided by many whites who feel themselves in a similar position. But Indian groups are themselves divided by factional disputes and seldom present a united front.

We might now return to Morgan in more systematic fashion and consider at greater length (1) his early experiences with the Iroquois, (2) his further observations on his field trips to the Missouri region, and (3) his more mature reflections, as they influenced his views as to the future of the American Indian. We shall see that, while some of his views were ethnocentric, others were quite realistic and form part of Indian Service policy even today. If he only hinted at the significance of an integrated sociocultural life for the maintenance of Indian unity, it was partly because he saw Indian life as breaking down under reservation conditions rather than being able to remodel itself around new values and activities.

II

Morgan published his *League of the Iroquois* in 1851, not only to give a scientific account of the government and social life of the Iroquois, but also—as he says—"to encourage a kinder feeling toward the Indian, founded upon a truer knowledge of his civil and domestic institutions, and of his capabilities for future elevation" (1851: ix). In the 1840's the frontier had moved well beyond Rochester, and the Iroquois had been dispossessed of all their lands in New York State, with the exception of a few remaining reservations which land speculators were eyeing hungrily.

The League, which could act only as a unit, had been divided with regard to the Revolutionary War, but most of the Iroquois honored their alliances and fought on the side of the British. As a result of the effectiveness of their raids on the border settlements, the Continental Congress sent an army under General Sullivan, in 1779, which destroyed their principal towns and burned their fields and orchards. The treaty of peace between Great Britain and the United States made no provision for the Iroquois, and a large group under the leadership of Joseph Brant, a Mohawk chief, sought the protection of Canada, who gave them a reservation on the Grand River, where their descendants still reside. Soon after, however, a general peace was established with the northwestern Indian nations, including the Iroquois. who from that time forth became "dependent nations."

In the next few years the Iroquois were overwhelmed by the tide of population moving westward. Within a decade after the first house was erected in Cayuga county, the whole Cayuga nation was uprooted and gone. The Seneca were the next to be overwhelmed and were able to retain only a few small reservations, which the Ogden Land Company was attempting to acquire through bribery and the lavish use of liquor. "It is no small crime against humanity," said Morgan, "to seize the fireside and property of a whole community, without an equivalent and against their will; and then to drive them, beggared and outraged into a wild and inhospitable wilderness" (1851: 33).

In the period of demoralization that followed the loss of their lands and autonomy, many of the Iroquois took to drink and violence or relapsed into apathy and idleness. About 1800, Handsome Lake, a Seneca sachem who had been in contact with Quaker missionaries, received a revelation from the Great Spirit commissioning him to preach a new religion among the Iroquois. Handsome Lake had earlier lived an idle and dissipated life, but after receiving his revelation he traveled from village to village preaching the new doctrine. The central teaching of the new religion was directed against the use of alcohol, and the Great Spirit had shown Handsome Lake a vision of the punishments reserved for drunkards and wife-beaters and the rewards to be found in the Indian heaven. After his death in 1815 his grandson was "raised up" as his successor and continued his teachings.

The new religion of Handsome Lake is now recognized as a "revitalization" movement, of a class with the Ghost Dance and other religious movements. Morgan was skeptical of the authenticity of the revelations but impressed with the results. He saw that Handsome Lake's doctrine not only "embodied all the precepts of the ancient faith, and recognized the ancient mode of worship, giving it anew the sanction of the Great Spirit, but it also comprehended such new doctrines as came in, very aptly, to lengthen out and enlarge the primitive system, without impairing the structure itself" (1851: 226). Morgan remarks on the credulity of the people and the chiefs, but notes that the influence of the new religion has probably saved them from extinction: "Its beneficent effects upon the people doubtless contributed more to its final establishment than any other cause" (1851: 231).

Today the teachings of Handsome Lake represent the *old* religion—the code by which the longhouse pagans and conservatives live on the various reservations in both the United States and Canada. It is not overtly anti-white, as the Ghost Dance became among the Sioux before their final defeat in 1890, but in the Indian heaven whites were excluded. There was one exception: George Washington, "Destroyer of villages," who had befriended the Iroquois after the Revolution, was allowed to live just outside the gates. In the recounting of the events, as recorded for Morgan by his friend and assistant, Ely S. Parker, the Messenger who guided Handsome Lake tells him:

The man you see is the only pale-face who ever left the earth. He was kind to you, when, on the settlement of the great difficulty between the Americans and the Great Crown, you were abandoned to the mercy of your enemies. This Crown told the Great American, that as for his allies, the Indians, he might kill them if he liked. The great American judged that this would be cruel and unjust. He believed they were made by the Great Spirit, and were entitled to the enjoyment of life. He was kind to you and extended over you his protection. For this reason he has been allowed to leave the earth. But he is never permitted to go into the presence of the Great Spirit. Although alone, he is perfectly happy. All faithful Indians pass him as they go to heaven. They see him, and recognize him, but pass on in silence. No word ever passes his lips [1851: 257].

For the Indians there was both a threat and a promise. If the people did not obey his commands, the Great Spirit would lose his patience and cause total darkness to spread over the earth and monsters and poisonous animals to emerge and kill the wicked. But before that happened he would take home to himself all the good and faithful.

Through the preaching of *gaiwiyoh*, "the good news," the Iroquois managed to live with defeat and subjection and to rise again from the demoralization of drunkenness and idleness to a position of moral superiority. In a recent study, "Cultural Composition of the Handsome Lake Religion" (1961), Anthony Wallace has discussed the major themes as constituting a blueprint of the ideal society and of how one should behave: the vices to be avoided, the obligations of kinship, the responsibilities to the community, political action, right religious belief and practice, desirable economic activities, and a policy of limited education. Within the context of the contact situation, Wallace sees the new religion shifting from reform to nativism and, ultimately, to an emotional identification with Indianness itself.

Morgan was only dimly aware of this social role of religion and its ability to maintain group integration under difficult conditions. Hence, as he discussed the future destiny of the Indian upon this continent, "the fact that he cannot be saved in his native state" seemed too obvious to need proof. "Civilization is aggressive, as well as progressive"—while Indian life is "a negative state without inherent vitality, and without powers of resistance." His solution for the reclaiming of the American Indian and for the ultimate civilization came from the recent history of the Iroquois:

> There are now about four thousand Iroquois living in the State of New York. Having for many years been surrounded by civilization, and shut in from all intercourse with the ruder tribes of the wilderness, they have not only lost their native fierceness, but have become quite tractable and humane. In addition to this, the agricultural pursuits into which they have gradually become initiated, have introduced new modes of life, and awakened new aspirations, until a change, in itself scarcely perceptible to the casual observer, but in reality very great, has been accomplished. At the present moment their decline has not only been arrested, but they are actually increasing in numbers. The proximate cause of this universal spectacle is to be found in their feeble attempts at agriculture; but the remote and the true one is to be discovered in the schools of the missionaries [1851: 446].

The lands of the Iroquois were still held in common, but

> their progress towards a higher agricultural life has rendered this ancient tenure a source of inconvenience; although they are not as yet prepared for their division among the people.... When the Iroquois reach such a stable position, as agriculturalists, as to make it safe to divide their lands among the several families of each nation, with the power of alienation, it will give to them that stimulus and ambition which separate rights of property are so well calculated to produce [1851: 455–56].

Morgan goes on to describe the various steps by which the Iroquois could safely come into possession of their rights to property and, ultimately, to the rights and privileges of citizenship. "When that time comes," he says, "They will cease to be Indians, except in name."

When Morgan wrote the *League of the Iroquois*, responsibility for the Indians had just been transferred from the Department of War to the Department of the Interior. "The present system of national supervision is evidently temporary in its plans and purposes, and designed for the administration of our Indian affairs with the least possible inconvenience," he writes. And the sentiment of the system is that *"the destiny of the Indian is extermination"* (1851: 457).

Morgan, who had helped the Seneca fight off the efforts of the Ogden Land Company to take over their reservations in the 1840's, would have been slightly incredulous if he could have returned a century later and found the Iroquois still fighting to retain their lands—this time against the encroachments of both state and federal government. For in the 1950's the Iroquois were fighting for their rights in the state and federal courts and hiring their own lawyers. The story of this decade is excellently told by Edmund Wilson in *Apologies to the Iroquois* (1959).

One of the projects discussed by Wilson is the Kinzua Dam, part of the Allegany Reservation Project passed by Congress in 1941 for flood control in the Ohio River Basin. The proposed dam, which would flood most of the habitable land on the Allegany reservation, was bitterly fought by the Seneca until 1959, when Congress authorized its construction by overriding a presidential veto. In this case the Seneca had a fair hearing by the standards of white law and were scheduled to receive financial compensation.

But, as three distinguished anthropologists pointed out in a memorandum to the subcommittees on Indian Affairs of the Senate and House of Representatives, recompense in money was not enough. Diamond, Sturtevant, and Fenton (1964: 63–33) emphasized that there were values among reservation Indians that were different from the prevailing usages in the larger society and that these values centered on land as the focus for Indian identity and as the basis for a network of economic, social, and ritual ties.

They go on to point out that

no matter how crude living and other facilities may be in fact, the reservation itself is a home and a shelter, and the most tangible symbol of Indianness, both for those now living there and for many tribe members temporarily living elsewhere. In this, Indians differ from other citizens, including other minority groups, for whom the specific land they occupy is of far less cultural and psychological significance.

They further note that no Indian in recent years has offered to sell his reservation lands.

III

During his series of field trips to the Missouri region in the years 1859–62, Morgan's perspective on the American Indian was both broadened and deepened. On the newly established reservations in Kansas-Nebraska Territory, he saw the agency system and mission activities at first hand, and he also sampled a wide range of frontier opinion. The new Indian agents, with the transfer of responsibility to the Department of the Interior, were political appointees rather than army officers, and they soon made "Indian affairs" synonymous with graft and corruption. Morgan reports (1959) that many agents were dishonest, some incompetent, and few really useful, and he noted the frequent tie-ins with traders, who were usually relatives, and the various techniques for robbing the Indians.

He found the experimental farms, which were designed to aid the transition to civilization, frequently run for the benefit of the agent. The crops were sold rather than distributed, machinery was hired out to white farmers, and the Indians "paid" in inflated goods. Later the agent might buy the farm through a confederate and retire at the expense of the Indians.

Above the agents in the more isolated regions loomed the American Fur Company, who controlled everything in the Indian country, and goods for free distribution often ended up for sale in the trading posts, and annuities destined for Indians were paid directly to the traders who had extended credit. Morgan saw part of the solution—the licensing of two or more traders for each region and separate paymasters—but the larger problem of adequate administration of Indian affairs is with us yet, though the situation is much improved.

The missions that Morgan saw on the frontier shook his faith in missionaries but not his view of the importance of mission schools. The Baptist Mission school for the Delawares, run by the Reverend John G. Pratt, excited his admiration: "This is the true system of Indian education, beyond a doubt, and this school is by far in the best condition of any I have seen" (1959: 54). But he found other missions that gave him pause: mission schools interested more in the $75 per child, which the government paid for room, board, and schooling, than in educating them, and missionaries who speculated in land and supplies along with the agents.

His faith in education still remained, however: "I think

the first and greatest blessing now which we can give the Indian is the English language" (1959: 101). It would make him independent; he could make himself understood and show the quality of his mind. Morgan thought the boarding school to be the only place where it could be done—"therefore I am for the missionary and the boarding school" (1959: 102).

Another problem that Morgan saw in new perspective on the frontier was that of race mixture. Some of the most intelligent Indian leaders that he met were mixed bloods, and he was particularly impressed with the favorable conditions for intermarriage in Kansas, where Indians from east of the Mississippi had been settled, along with Prairie tribes:

I think an amalgamation with the Indians by the white race, or the absorption of the best blood of their race into our own, is destined to take place, and that Kansas will be the theater of the first honest and regular experiment. Hitherto the lowest and basest whites have been the fathers of the half breeds. Now we are to see respectable white people marry the daughters of wealthy and respectable Indians and bring up their children with the advantages of education, Christianity, and wealth. . . . [1959: 42].

He thought our race would be toughened physically and benefited mentally, but the Kansas settlers did not wait to find out; they brought about a further removal of the Indians to Indian Territory as rapidly as possible.

The deleterious effects of race mixture were to be seen in the vicinity of the army posts, where few unions were permanent and thousands of half-breed children grew up without fathers. Later, when Morgan visited the Red River settlements, where some ten thousand persons of mixed Orkney Islander Scots and Cree Indian descent were living, he was interested in the question whether the mixed stock could perpetuate itself. He came to the conclusion that the half-blood was inferior to the pure Indian but that further crosses were advantageous, a conclusion that is dubious biologically but possibly correct sociologically.

The common frontier view that the only way to tame an Indian is to put white blood in his veins brought an interesting response from Morgan:

I think a most important idea lies in here and it is one that has occurred to me before; and that is, whether after all it is not in virtue of the white blood already taken up and distributed among the emigrant nations [that] the improvement we see among them has come to pass; and that for this blood all efforts would have been unavailable to introduce agriculture among them. I can hardly think it true and yet it may be [1959: 94].

On the Indian reservations in Kansas, Morgan found Indian tribes in all stages of progress, as evidenced by agricultural advancement, white dress, and schooling. The Ottawas, a small group originally from Canada and closely related to the Ojibwa and Potawatomi, had been removed from Ohio in 1836. They were far advanced and anxious to divide up their land into individual allotments, but the Secretary of the Interior had refused his concurrence, so they had gone ahead and divided the land without the aid or consent of the government. Morgan considered that:

Their desire to divide their lands and the assurance they feel that they can do so and keep their farms, is quite encouraging. I confess I am afraid of it, but it may be that they can bear it. It must come to that with every Indian nation, or they must be exterminated. When they can become farmers and each own and sell his own farm, then the stimulus to exertion which they so much need will be applied and it may make good farmers of a share of them, and thus save a portion. They must also change their government and have a council, and allow no man to sell his land to a white or an Indian without the consent of the Council [1959: 38].

The Ottawas had already lost their clans and given up all pagan practices for the white mode of life, and they were hoping to get a school. Morgan, who had put his faith in education, was puzzled as to how they had done it all without a school or a boarding house among them.

On the Shawnee reservation, where there were competing missions, Morgan found the Shawnees already "trying the great and dangerous experiment of dividing up their lands, with the unrestrained power of sale in each individual" (1959: 44–45). They originally had 100,000 acres of the best-watered land in Kansas, but with the rapid settlement of the territory, he says, "the Shawnees appear to have been wise enough to see the necessity of removing or selling a large part of their reserve lest they should find their condition intolerable from the pressure upon them by the whites." But the Shawnee were used to being moved from pillar to post and would soon depart for other territories.

The Delawares were also advanced in agriculture, with well-timbered lands and a large annuity, and Morgan (1959: 55) saw no reason why some of them should not become both agriculturalists and respected citizens of the state, their children intermarrying with the whites. The residue he foresaw as being run out or forced into the mountain regions.

These and other observations gave Morgan a better perspective on Indian problems. He would not live until the period of wholesale allotments of the late nineteenth century and later, which led to the breaking-up of Indian Territory and throwing it open to white settlement and ultimate statehood, but he saw both the virtues and the perils of the process. In much of Oklahoma the processes of assimilation and acculturation have operated to destroy the Indian and create a citizen, though Indian life continues in modified fashion in marginal areas. In this process whole tribes have become "extinct" as groups, though their genes are present in the larger population.

Morgan also found Indians who denounced the annuity system. One prominent Ottawa leader thought it would be better to give the principal to the Indians and let them waste it and then be compelled to rely on themselves—if it could be used for no better purposes than it was now. Some of our officials now believe in theory that Indians can learn to administer their own resources only by making occasional mistakes, but it is seldom practiced.

As a result of his conversations with various Indian leaders, Morgan believed that the time was at hand to reverse the government policy toward the Indians. He learned that the Indians were discussing the consolidation of remnant tribes into a single group with a common territory and a new form of government:

A convention of the most sensible men has been proposed and within a year or two we may witness it. Great results would flow from it. Our people would be astonished at the amount of ability and experience and wisdom these nations, broken and scattered as they are, could assemble. . . . Such a convention would be a new and great event in the history of the Indian [1959: 38].

But such a convention had to wait almost exactly one hundred years, until the American Indian Conference was held at Chicago, June 13–20, 1961, and issued a "Declaration of Purpose," which recommended a course of action for American Indian policy.

IV

Morgan's experiences on the frontier convinced him of the necessity for a different policy toward the Indian, and he began to look toward Washington, D.C. Lincoln had been nominated by the newly formed Republican party, and, according to Carl Resek:

Anticipating Lincoln's election, Morgan thought it conceivable that he might be appointed the next Commissioner of Indian Affairs. The conditions in Kansas convinced him that a trained ethnologist and an honest man was needed in the Indian office. It was imperative to clean out the corruption and to establish schools to train the Indians in agricultural and manufacturing techniques. It was also his one chance to become a professional scientist, the Bache of ethnology. Since his last application for a federal appointment, he had learned a few rules of politics [1960: 82].

He entered the New York state assembly, became chairman of its Committee on Indian Affairs, and solicited letters of recommendation from his friends and associates. He was very likely the best qualified candidate, but Lincoln's campaign manager had promised the position to an Indiana politician who had swung the state to Lincoln. Morgan's supporters urged him to continue his efforts, but, while he ran for state senator a few years later, he largely abandoned politics and returned to his ethnological studies.

When Grant was elected President, hope flared anew, and Morgan applied for a foreign mission, but again he lost out. However, Grant did appoint his former aide, and Morgan's protegé, Ely S. Parker, as Commissioner of Indian Affairs, and Morgan had high hopes for a change. But the scandal and the corruption of the Grant regime did not spare the Indian department, and Parker was forced to resign after two years.

The publication of *Systems of Consanguinity* (1871) brought Morgan into public notice and established him as a major American scholar. He took his family on a grand tour of Europe, where he met Darwin, Lubbock, Maine, and McLennan. He then returned to continue his research and writing. The ideas that he was later to present in *Ancient Society* (1877) began to take form, the great ethnic periods—savagery, barbarism, and civilization—were clarified and subdivided, and the "laws" that governed man's progress were laid down. He criticized the historians, particularly Bancroft, for taking the tales of the Spanish chroniclers too seriously and writing about empires and rulers. The Aztecs, after all, were barbarians, and their organization was nothing more than the Iroquois confederacy—writ large. During this period he was introduced to a young scholar named Bandelier by the then president of the University of Rochester, who under Morgan's guidance began the revision of Mexican ethnology and history.

By 1875 Morgan was the acknowledged leader of American ethnology. In that year he established the Section on Anthropology of the American Association for the Advancement of Science (of which he became president a few years later) and was elected to the National Academy of Sciences. Of later anthropologists only Franz Boas was similarly honored. He now became an international figure, and scholars came to Rochester to discuss their research plans and results.

The defeat of General Custer and the loss of his entire command at the hands of the Sioux and their allies in 1876 brought Morgan back to the Indian problem. In a long letter to the *Nation* (July 20, 1876) he defended the Sioux, pointing out that Custer had experienced the precise fate he had intended for the Indians. And, summarizing the recent history of Sioux relations, he noted that the United States government had begun the war.

He also called attention to the continued absence of any systematic program for the administration of Indian affairs and urged the creation of a Department of Indian Affairs, with cabinet rank, to be put in the hands of some outstanding man.

Morgan had earlier, in 1862, sent a series of proposals for the revision of Indian policy and the reform of the Indian department to President Lincoln, in which he had suggested the creation of separate Indian territories, one for the eastern tribes and one for the Plains Indians. Now (1876) he returned to these proposals and suggested a "factory" system for the reservations and a "pastoral" system for the still-wild tribes. The Plains Indians, who could raise and winter horses, could be taught to raise and winter herds of cattle as a substitute for the vanished buffalo. Since the government was obligated by treaty to furnish the Indians cattle for food, this system would be economical, in that they would raise their own supply and ultimately furnish the East with meat as well.

This proposal had been put into practice independently by General Mackenzie, who had rounded up a band of Comanches and sold their horses, purchasing sheep with the proceeds. "The Indians seem much pleased with the experiment," a correspondent wrote to the *Nation,* but the Comanches were not shepherds for long.

The "factory" system was for more advanced tribes, who, as "barbarians," were still below the plane of civilization and whose industry needed stimulation "since the love of property is still a feeble passion." Morgan described an experiment among the Ojibwa near Sault Ste Marie, where a missionary had successfully organized groups of Indians to make raspberry jam, birch-bark ornaments, mats, maple sugar, and moccasins for the tourist trade. What was needed was a "factor" to find a market for the Indian products and keep a watch on design. He believed the Indian women "would solve the problem in every Indian tribe and raise the Indians gradually into a vastly improved condition, if given a fair chance."

Morgan returned to these proposals in his final communication on the "Indian question" to the *Nation* in 1878, when Congress was being urged to transfer the Indians back to the Department of War. He reiterated the "total failure" of the present system and the need for a Department of Indian Affairs and suggested again the virtues of the "factor" system and the "pastoral" system. The new evolutionary theories, recently presented in *Ancient Society,* were invoked to explain the failure of the Indians to progress. We might quote Morgan again:

We wonder that our Indians cannot civilize, but how could they, any more than our own remote barbarous ancestors jump ethnical periods? They have the skulls and brains of barbarians and must grow toward civilization as all mankind has done who attained to it by a progressive experience [1878: 332].

By natural "law" progress is slow and regular, and we

must plan to put the Indians through the proper stages before we can expect them to attain to civilization—so runs the argument.

But in Mexico and Central America, and in the Andes as well, civilization had already been achieved by Indians related to those we have surveyed and not different in race from Morgan's Iroquois. And Morgan's own observations on the Indian frontier challenged his new theories.

In retrospect it is easy to see where Morgan went astray. His stages of cultural evolution were a reflex of the evolutionary temper of the times and were based on a logical formulation that he had largely constructed rather than on a piecing-together of the evidence from the past. Today, those who concern themselves with social and cultural evolution make a distinction between macro-evolution and microevolution and do not expect the cultures of individual tribes to recapitulate the trends they see in culture as a whole. For Morgan, culture and race were linked somehow through the processes of inheritance, and man, while subject to natural "law," was not a product of Darwinian evolution. The clarification of the nature of culture and its social inheritance did not come until Edward B. Tylor's *Primitive Culture*, in 1871, and by then Morgan's own thinking had progressed in different directions. His ethnocentrism and his faith in progress he also shared with Americans of the nineteenth century. Perhaps because he led his contemporaries so well, he became the central target for the critical reaction of the decades to follow.

V

Today the Indian problem is still with us, despite an ever increasing bureaucracy and budget, and the attempted solutions are still very much the same as in Morgan's time. You will recall his prediction, in 1878, that the Indians and their posterity "will live in our midst for centuries to come" and the reasons he proposed: the persistence and effectiveness of their arts for the maintenance of life and their standing apart from our social and political system.

Since 1920 the Indian population has been increasing from a low point at the turn of the century to more than 500,000 Indians at the present time. We have noted the policy changes with recent administrations: John Collier's "new deal" for the Indians, the postwar policy of termination of federal controls, and the recent shift to economic development of reservation resources. One of President Kennedy's first acts was to appoint a Task Force on Indian Affairs, headed by W. W. Keeler, who is both principal chief of the Cherokee Nation and executive vice-president of the Phillip's Petroleum Company, and its report stressed the following related objectives: (1) maximum Indian economic self-sufficiency, (2) full participation of Indians in American life, and (3) equal citizenship privileges and responsibilities. The Task Force Report (1961: 8) recognized that the support of the Indian communities is vital to the attainment of these objectives and believed that "the Indians can retain their tribal identities and much of their culture while working toward a greater adjustment and, for the further enrichment of our society, it is in our best interests to do so."

At the same time, the American Indian Chicago Conference was convened in June, 1961, with some 460 Indians from 90 tribes, and their recommendations were considerably different. They asked for the return of Indian lands and the enlargement of their reservations, as well as protection of Indian rights and privileges against the encroachments of both state and federal governments. They were particularly concerned with their treaty rights as self-governing, though dependent, groups. To quote from "A Declaration of Indian Purpose":

In our day, each remaining acre is a promise that we will still be here tomorrow. Were we paid a thousand times the market value of our lost holdings, still the payment would not suffice. Money never mothered the Indian people, as the land has mothered them, nor have any people become more closely attached to the land, religiously and traditionally.

But, above all, they asked for understanding as they struggle to hold to identity and survival—"to regain in the America of the space age some measure of the adjustment they enjoyed as the original possessors of their native land."

Not all the Indians have agreed to these objectives. As we have seen, about one-third of the Indian population are no longer on reservations and are making their way in the white world. But some two-thirds of the Indians still prefer reservation life, despite its well-known difficulties. To the social anthropologist the reasons are clear. Man does not live by jobs alone, but in society. On the reservation the Indian is surrounded by kinsmen and friends, and patterns of sharing remove some of the hazards of existence. And there are rituals to maintain the relation between man and nature, as well as between man and man. The Indian who ventures into the white world meets with good will but also with race and class prejudice. But as Indian communities form in the cities they create again a society in which they can live.

How far this process can go is vividly illustrated by the Narragansetts, who once numbered several thousands in the mid-1650's and occupied most of present-day Rhode Island. Today the Narragansett tribe is not distinguishable by racial characteristics or by any aboriginal traits or values. But they have been able to maintain unity and group identity through a combination of institutions: (1) the tribal organization and its meetings, (2) the annual powwow and similar "ceremonial" undertakings, and (3) the Indian church and its management. Here, extremely acculturated individuals maintain themselves as an organized group to emphasize their Indian identity and to preserve a continuity with the past, as they see it.

On a national scale the growing Pan Indian movement is utilizing similar institutions for similar purposes. Dancing, once used for ceremonial purposes, still performs a social function, and the Native American Church is gaining adherents as the local rituals are abandoned. At the political level the National Congress of American Indians is beginning to speak with a single voice. As the Indian begins to understand *us*, he is shifting from passive accommodation to our desires to an active concern for his own future. The events over which we feel the greatest guilt are the ones from which the Indian draws his greatest strength.

Today, the Bureau of Indian Affairs is engaged in a great effort to develop Indian resources on the reservation and off. Education of Indian children is still the major activity, but in the last decade there has developed an extensive program of vocational training for a wide variety of jobs. In addition, there is now under way an intensive effort to develop mineral resources, forest products, irrigation, roads, and industry on the reservation, as well as an effort to bring the Indians up to modern standards of health.

The program is in the hands of a Commissioner of Indian Afairs, Philleo Nash, who is trained as an anthropologist and who has had extensive experience both in our federal government and in our state system. His policy is to implement the recommendations of the Task Force, of which he was a member, but he proposes to do so by "moving away from the all-pervasive paternalism of the 1880's and 90's toward a more wholesome respect for the human dignity of individual Indians as well as for the values of age-old tribal cultures."

There is not one "Indian problem," but many—as many as there are Indian tribes or groups. Each is different in important respects, though there are also common features. In the past we have often attempted to solve these problems by a single formula, where a flexible program was required. But the basic conflict between the goal of full participation in American life and maintenance of Indian identity is a difficult problem to solve in the American scene. We find it hard to treat societies as different but equal—differences are usually evaluated as superior and inferior.

In the last analysis, it is the Indians themselves who will solve their problems. There is currently a great ferment on many reservations and increased communication between different Indian groups and between Indians and whites. Out of this dialogue will come a greater realization that the future of the Indians is in their hands and that they need to make the basic decisions. For it is their *dependent* status that is their greatest problem, as it is in all the new nations.

VII

EPILOGUE

I

IN THIS SERIES OF LECTURES WE HAVE NOT ATTEMPTED TO
evaluate Lewis H. Morgan in any systematic fashion but
have largely let him speak for himself. There are eulogies
aplenty in our learned journals, and much criticism as
well, and we have quoted some of both. But in living
imaginatively with Morgan during these recent months,
I have developed a greater appreciation of his accomplishments and hope that I have managed to convey something
of his anthropological personality.

After a long period of neglect, Morgan is coming to
be appreciated, not only for his contributions to social and
cultural evolution, which have been both severely criticized and strongly defended, but for his pioneer studies
of kinship and social organization. His *Systems of Consanguinity and Affinity of the Human Family* (1871),
which Goldenweiser called "one of the most famous, if
least read, works in the entire field of ethnology" (1915:
350), has in recent decades stimulated—directly or indirectly—enough research on social organization that we
are much closer to having the data to justify the title.

We have attempted in the preceding chapters to restore Morgan to the position that Lévi-Strauss has given him: the founder of kinship studies and the comparative study of society, which today we call social anthropology. You will recall that Lévi-Strauss, with regard to kinship, emphasized its permanency, systematic character, and continuity of changes. The permanency that Morgan envisaged with regard to his broad types is no longer acceptable, though particular patterns are often highly stable and may have a long life span. He was partly led astray by the new geological time scale, which was supplanting the biblical estimates. In the Preface to *Ancient Society* (1877), he notes that the great antiquity of mankind has been established and that man is now known to have existed in Europe in the glacial period. "One hundred or two hundred thousand years would be an unextravagent estimate of the period from the disappearance of the glaciers in the northern hemisphere to the present time." Today we restrict this period to some ten thousand years.

The systematic character of kinship is still basic to our thinking, though we have enlarged our conception of the kinship system to include not only the terminological patterns but also the behavior expectable or occurring between relatives. And, while we still begin with the genealogical base in the study of kinship, today we emphasize the *social recognition* of these and other categories. We have also developed more adequate classifications of kinship systems since Morgan's early attempts, and we are beginning to understand the role of preferential and prescriptive marriage patterns and the significance of affinity.

But it is with regard to the problems of change in social

systems that we have made the greatest progress. Morgan conceived of change in kinship systems as the result of broad changes in the nature of human society, and particularly in its forms of marriage. This was a "functional" explanation on a macroscopic scale, which had a certain logic but which ran aground with regard to the ethnographic evidence. In the Mountain Province of the Philippines, for example, there are groups, such as the Ifugao, with a "Malayan" type of kinship system side by side with groups, such as the Bontok and Kalinga, with systems much like our own. And one group, at least, the Sagada Igorots, uses a "descriptive" system for reference and a "Malayan" system in direct address. Here almost the whole gamut of Morgan's social evolution is encompassed in one group.

The foregoing chapters represent one approach to the study of change in social systems. Murdock (1949) has pioneered a more analytic and statistical approach, which has had important results and has enabled him to present a preliminary survey of "North American Social Organization" (1955) that

leads to the inescapable conclusion that the North American Indians are basically characterized by social systems of bilateral type and have acquired unilinear systems only here and there, not through any single evolutionary process, nor through successive waves of diffusion, but independently in widely separated regions in response to peculiarly favorable local conditions [1955: 95].

And Spicer and his collaborators, in *Perspectives in American Indian Culture Change* (1961), have begun to deal with the complexities of culture-contact situations and the resulting processes of culture change in terms of documentary and other records.

We have attempted to make progress by concentrating our attention on change in the social system, utilizing kinship as one important aspect, and attempting to control as many factors as possible. What we have done does not add up to a theory of social change as yet, but it does contain some of the essential ingredients. In our chapter on the Southeast we dealt in simplified terms with the effects of white pressures on the Choctaw and other tribes after their removal to Indian Territory. Spoehr's more detailed researches defined the contact agents more adequately and illustrated the steps by which the overall changes actually occurred. And Bruner's microscopic analysis of change in similar social systems, but in another area, suggests some of the dynamics of the actual processes.

There were, of course, many other changes going on in the tribes of the Southeast that we have not considered here. Thus Fred Gearing, in *Priests and Warriors, Social Structures for Cherokee Politics in the 18th Century* (1962), has considered in detail the internal social and political changes brought about by the pressures of English and French colonists and the requirements for survival. William S. Willis, Jr., has argued (1963) that patrilineal institutions were probably widespread in the Southeast in addition to the matrilineal institutions Spoehr and I have dealt with, and has presented a number of examples of patrilineal inheritance of chieftainship during the eighteenth century as supporting evidence. It is clear that white "models" were important in the Southeast during the colonial period and that much political acculturation occurred during this period, as well as later, But, except for the well-known patrilineal societies of the Yuchi, which may be aboriginal, I see little evidence for the existence of patrilineal *institutions*. The close affectional relations of fathers and sons in matrilineal societies and the conflicts they engender are well known—Malinowski's Trobriand chiefs are a famous example. But for the Southeast I offer Edward's statement with regard to Choctaw chiefs:

> When the missionaries went among them in 1819 they had three chiefs, one to each of three districts, into which the nation was divided. This office was hereditary, yet not in what we would consider the direct line. The chief's son could not have it. His nephew, that is, his sister's son was the heir apparent [1932: 395].

The missionaries soon changed this situation for the Choctaw by introducing elections. And at least some of the cases cited by Willis refer to chiefs created at the behest of white authorities, for whom there was no traditional pattern of inheritance.

In the Plains we have been more concerned with ecological factors in relation both to patterns of subsistence and to forms of social organization. Here the reservation period has been more recent and has not been studied in detail, except for a few instances. We have emphasized the important distinction between the High Plains and the Prairie Plains, so far as social organization is concerned, and have been particularly interested in what happens to social systems as groups move from one area into the other. Of particular significance is our finding that groups moving into the High Plains from different regions and with different social and cultural organizations came to approximate a single High Plains type. The shifts in technology were not so great and have long been accepted. But the shifts in social structure, and particularly in kinship patterns, should be of interest to scholars who have conceived of kinship terminology as primarily linguistic phenomena. Here, also, we find more complex unilineal structures reverting to the basic pattern that Murdock (1955: 95) believes to characterize the social systems of the American Indians.

In the Great Lakes region we have been concerned with both ecology and the influence of patterns of preferential marriage, as well as with white acculturation and the interaction of Indian group with Indian group. Here there is an interesting relationship between cross-cousin marriage and the clan organization. From north to south, among the Ojibwa and other Central Algonkians, as the intensity of cross-cousin marriage increases, the strength and importance of the lineage organization decreases, and as the strength of the lineage organization increases, cross-cousin marriage tends to disappear. We have seen that the development of "corporate" groupings among the Central Algonkians has resulted in an organization comparable to that of the Central Siouans. And Callender's careful study of the surviving Central Algonkian tribes has made it possible to see the modern systems as variants of an earlier structure, as affected by white acculturation and other historical factors. In the north we have found groups that moved out onto the plains and utilized the buffalo going through demographic and social changes similar to those occurring *in situ* when the family-allowance system of the Canadian government improved the economic position of the Berens River Ojibwa. Hallowell's attempt to see the social systems of the northern Algonkians as variations of a basic pattern under the influence of acculturation and new conditions has been the key to our understanding of much of what has happened in the Great Lakes region.

In the Southwest we have considered only a few of the many problems that attract the social anthropologist. The Southwest is almost the last region where American Indian life continues in neo-aboriginal form, and the patterns of secrecy of the Pueblo populations make it a region of continuing interest. Here we were concerned with the problem of explaining the differences between the social systems of the eastern and western Pueblos in the light of their great cultural similarities. With regard to this problem the archeological record will be crucial, and we have indicated above some of the preliminary findings.

The Southern Athabaskans offer another opportunity to study social change under a combination of acculturation to Pueblo groups and adaptation to new ecological niches in the Southwest—as well as on the Plains and in Oregon and California—and a number of studies have already been made. Here there have been important changes in both the cultural patterns and the social systems, along with the retention of certain basic value patterns.

With regard to the Indians generally, we have called attention to the remarkable survival of Indian populations, as well as the absorption of many groups into the larger society. Morgan's prediction that the Indians would be with us for a long time have come true partly because of the strength and resiliency of their social systems and partly because of the survival of Indian values.

We have considered only a part of the data now available on the American Indian, but what we have done with this sample suggests that social and cultural change, while far more complex than Morgan envisaged, has certain regularities that make it well worth studying. In broad perspective, Morgan saw the American Indian system as growing out of the Malayan and evolving toward the European "descriptive" system. Murdock suggests that bilateral "Hawaiian"-type systems are basic to the American Indian and have developed independently here and there into unilinear systems. My own view is that there has been an alternation between "generation" and "lineage" systems of a cyclical character, with generational systems developing "lineage" specializations under favorable circumstances and "breaking down" into bilateral systems of one subtype or another when ecological or other conditions change. In such generalizations we are not so far from Morgan.

ii

It might be worth noting, in conclusion, that Morgan made considerable sacrifices, both personal and financial, in carrying out his field researches. The financial costs he was well able to maintain, since he had extensive investments in Michigan and elsewhere. But the loss of his two daughters was a different matter. On his last trip up the Missouri in 1862, en route to the Rocky Mountains, he received word that one of his daughters was ill of diphtheria. In an agony of indecision he decided to go on, but the prospect of her death or recovery hung over him throughout the rest of the journey, though seldom mentioned in his journal. On the return trip, almost two months later, he received the news that both his daughters had succumbed. He ends his *Indian Journals,* July 3, 1862, with the statement:

Two out of three of my children are taken. The intelligence has simply petrified me. I have not shed a tear. It is too profound for tears. Thus ends my last expedition. I go home to my stricken and mourning wife, a miserable and destroyed man [1959: 200].

But he rallied from his despair and went on to complete *Systems*, which he attempted, without success, to dedicate to his two daughters. This loss may well have led Morgan to devote the rest of his life to science, and his gift to the University of Rochester for the education of women is in their memory.

At the Morgan Centennial Celebration, held at Wells College, Aurora, in June, 1919, a tablet was presented to the college commemorating the one-hundredth anniversary of his birth and containing a quotation from *Ancient Society* that gave his vision of the world:

Democracy in government, brotherhood in society, equality in rights and privileges and universal education foreshadow the next higher plane of society to which experience, intelligence and knowledge are steadily tending. It will be a revival in a higher form of the liberty, equality and fraternity of the ancient gentes.

Read either in evolutionary terms or in terms of mankind's struggle to achieve a satisfying life, it is a vision that has significance for the modern world. Morgan's Iroquois had it in one form, and we are currently trying to attain it, not only for ourselves, but for all races and peoples.

BIBLIOGRAPHY

AMERICAN INDIAN CONFERENCE
    1961   A declaration of Indian purpose. Proceedings of the American Indian Chicago Conference, The University of Chicago, June 13-20, 1961. (Mimeographed)

ANASTASIO, A.
    n.d.   Intergroup relations in the Southern Plateau. Unpublished Ph.D. thesis, University of Chicago, 1955.

BENEDICT, R.
    1934   Patterns of culture. Boston and New York, Houghton Mifflin Co.

BOAS, F.
    1896   The limitations of the comparative method in anthropology. Science, n.s. 4: 901–908. (reprinted in F. Boas, Race, language and culture. New York, Macmillan Co., 1940).

BOTT, E.
    n.d.   A comparison of the social organization of the the Emo and Ponemah bands of Ojibwa Indians. Unpublished M.A. thesis, University of Chicago, 1949.

BRUNER, E.
    1955   Two processes of change in Mandan-Hidatsa kinship terminology. American Anthropologist 57: 840–50.
    1956   Primary group experience and the processes of acculturation. American Anthropologist 58: 605–23.

179

CALLENDER, C.
1962   The social organization of the Central Algonkians. Milwaukee Public Museum, Publications in Anthropology, no. 7. Milwaukee, Wis.

CARVER, J.
1796   Travels through the interior parts of North America in the years 1766, 1767, and 1768. Philadelphia.

CONNELLY, J. C.
n.d.   Clan-lineage relations in a Pueblo village phratry. Unpublished M.A. Thesis, University of Chicago, 1956.

COOPER, A.
n.d.   Ecological aspects of the family hunting territory system of the northeastern Algonkians. Unpublished M.A. Thesis, University of Chicago, 1942.

DEBO, A.
1934   The rise and fall of the Choctaw Republic. Norman, University of Oklahoma Press.

DEETZ, J.
n.d.   An archaeological approach to kinship change in eighteenth century Arikara culture. Ph.D. thesis, Harvard University, 1960. (See Abstract 368, Abstracts of New World archaeology, ed. R. B. Woodbury, vol. 2, 1960. Society for American Archaeology, 1961).

DIAMOND, S., W. C. STURTEVANT, and W. N. FENTON
1964   Memorandum submitted to Subcommittees on Indian Affairs of the Senate and House of Representatives. American Anthropologist 66: 631–33.

DOLE, G. E., and R. L. CARNEIRO (eds.)
1960   Essays in the science of culture in honor of Leslie A. White. New York, Thomas Y. Crowell Co.

DOZIER, E. P.
1954   The Hopi-Tewa of Arizona. Berkeley and Los Angeles, University of California Press.
1960   The Pueblos of the south-western United States.

Journal of the Royal Anthropological Institute 90: 146–60.

1961   Rio Grande Pueblos. *In* Perspectives in American Indian culture change, ed. E. Spicer, pp. 94–186. Chicago, University of Chicago Press.

DUNNING, R. W.

1959   Social and economic change among the northern Ojibwa. Toronto, University of Toronto Press.

EDWARDS, J.

1932   The Choctaw Indians in the middle of the nineteenth century. Chronicles of Oklahoma, vol. 10, no. 3, Oklahoma City, pp. 392–425.

EGGAN, F.

1937   The Cheyenne and Arapaho kinship systems. *In* Social anthropology of North American tribes, ed. F. Eggan, pp. 35–95. Chicago, University of Chicago Press.

1937b   Historical changes in the Choctaw kinship system. American Anthropologist 39: 34–52.

1950   Social organization of the western Pueblos. Chicago, University of Chicago Press.

1952   The ethnological cultures and their archeological backgrounds. *In* Archeology of the eastern United States, ed. J. B. Griffin, pp. 34–45. Chicago, University of Chicago Press.

1955   Social anthropology: methods and results. *In* Social anthropology of North American tribes, ed. F. Eggan, pp. 485–551. Enlarged edition. Chicago, University of Chicago Press.

1960   Lewis H. Morgan in kinship perspective. *In* Essays in the science of culture in honor of Leslie A. White, ed. G. E. Dole and R. L. Carneiro, pp. 179–201. New York, Thomas Y. Crowell Co.

1965   Lewis H. Morgan and the future of the American Indian. Proceedings of the American Philosophical Society 109: 272–76. Philadelphia.

EGGAN, F. (ed.)

1937   Social anthropology of North American tribes. Chicago, University of Chicago Press.

1955   *Ibid.* Enlarged edition.

ELLIS, F. H., and J. J. BRODY
    1964   Ceramic stratigraphy and tribal history at Taos
                Pueblo. American Antiquity 29, no. 3: 316–27.

FISCHER, J. L.
    1964   Solutions for the Natchez paradox. Ethnology
                3, no. 1: 53–65.

FOREMAN, G.
    1934   The five civilized tribes. Norman, University of
                Oklahoma Press.

FORTUNE, R.
    1932   Omaha secret societies. Columbia University,
                Contributions to Anthropology, no. 14. New
                York.

FREIRE-MARRECO, B.
    1914   Tewa kinship terms from the Pueblo of Hano,
                Arizona. American Anthropologist 16: 269–87.

GEARING, F.
    1962   Priests and warriors, social structures for Chero-
                kee politics in the 18th century. American
                Anthropological Association, Memoir 93. Mena-
                sha, Wis.

GILBERT, W. H., JR.
    n.d.   Eastern Cherokee social organization. Ph.D.
                thesis, University of Chicago, 1934.
    1937   Eastern Cherokee social organization. *In* Social
                anthropology of North American tribes, ed. F.
                Eggan, pp. 285–340. Chicago, University of
                Chicago Press.

GOGGIN, J. M., and W. C. STURTEVANT
    1964   The Calusa: A stratified, nonagricultural society.
                In Explorations in cultural anthropology: essays
                in honor of George Peter Murdock, ed. W. H.
                Goodenough, pp. 179–220. New York, McGraw-
                Hill Co.

GOLDENWEISER, A. A.
    1915   Social organization of the North American
                Indians. *In* Anthropology in North America, ed.
                F. Boas, *et al.*, pp. 350–78. New York, G. F.
                Stechert & Co.

GOODENOUGH, W. H. (ed.)
  1964   Explorations in cultural anthropology: essays
              in honor of George Peter Murdock. New York,
              McGraw-Hill Co.

HAAS, M.
  1939   Natchez and Chitimacha clans and kinship
              terminology. American Anthropologist 41: 597–
              610.
  1958   A new linguistic relationship in North America:
              Algonkian and the Gulf languages. Southwestern
              Journal of Anthropology. 14, no. 3: 231–64.

HALLOWELL, A. I.
  1930   Was cross-cousin marriage formerly practiced by
              the North-Central Algonkian? Proceedings of
              the XXIII International Congress of American-
              ists, pp. 519–44. New York.
  1937   Cross-cousin marriage in the Lake Winnipeg
              area. *In* Publications of the Philadelphia An-
              thropological Society, ed. D. S. Davidson, vol. 1,
              pp. 95–110. Philadelphia.

HASSRICK, R.
  1944   The Teton Dakota kinship system. American
              Anthropologist 46: 338–47.

HAURY, E. W.
  1950   The stratigraphy and archaeology of Ventana
              Cave, Arizona. Albuquerque and Tucson, Uni-
              versity of New Mexico Press and University of
              Arizona Press.

HAURY, E. W. (ed.)
  1954   The Southwest issue. American Anthropologist
              56: 529–731.

HAWLEY, F. (see also ELLIS, F. H.)
  1937   Pueblo social organization as a lead to Pueblo
              history. American Anthropologist 39: 504–22.

HICKERSON, H.
  1962   The Southwestern Chippewa, an ethnohistorical
              study. American Anthropological Association,
              Memoir 92. Menasha, Wis.

HOCKETT, C. F.
  1964   The Proto Central Algonquian kinship system.

In Explorations in cultural anthropology, ed. W. H. Goodenough, pp. 239–58. New York: McGraw-Hill Co.

HONIGMANN, J. J.
1949   Culture and ethos of Kaska society. Yale University Publications in Anthropology, no. 40. New Haven, Conn.

HOWARD, J. H.
1960   The cultural position of the Dakota: a reassessment. *In* Essays in the science of culture in honor of Leslie A. White, ed. G. E. Dole and R. L. Carneiro, pp. 249–68. New York, Thomas Y. Crowell Co.
1963–64   The Plains-Ojibwa or Bungi. Museum News, University of South Dakota, vols. 24–25. Vermillion, S.D.

JENNINGS, J. D.
1957   Danger Cave. University of Utah Anthropological Papers, no. 27. Salt Lake City, Utah.

JOHNSON, F. (ed.)
1946   Man in northeastern North America. Papers of the R. S. Peabody Foundation for Archaeology, vol. 3. Andover, Mass.

KROEBER, A. L.
1909   Classificatory systems of relationship. Journal of the Royal Anthropological Institute 39: 77–84. London.
1939   Cultural and natural areas of native North America. Berkeley, University of California Press.

LAFITAU, J. F.
1724   Moeurs des Sauvages Américains. Paris.

LANDES, R.
1935   The Santee or eastern Dakota. Manuscript in possession of the author.
1936   The Potawatomi. Manuscript in possession of the author.
1937   Ojibwa sociology. Columbia University, Contributions to Anthropology, vol. 29. New York.

LESSER, A.
    1929   Kinship origins in the light of some distributions. American Anthropologist 31: 710-30.

    1930   Some aspects of Siouan kinship. Proceedings of the XXIII International Congress of Americanists, pp. 463–71. New York.

LÉVI-STRAUSS, C.
    1953   Social structure. *In* Anthropology today: an encyclopedic inventory, prepared under the chairmanship of A. L. Kroeber, pp. 524–53. Chicago, University of Chicago Press.

    1963   Potawatomi medicine. Transactions of the Kansas Academy of Science, vol. 66, no. 4: 553–99.

LONGACRE, W.
    1964   Archeology as anthropology: a case study. Science 144: 1454–55.

LOUNSBURY, F.
    1956   A semantic analysis of the Pawnee kinship usage. Language 32: 158–94.

    1964   A formal account of the Crow- and Omaha-type kinship terminologies. *In* Explorations in cultural anthropology, ed. W. H. Goodenough, pp. 351–93. New York, McGraw-Hill Co.

LOWIE, R. H.
    1914   Social organization. American Journal of Sociology 20: 68–97.

    1917   The kinship systems of the Crow and Hidatsa. Proceedings of the XIX International Congress of Americanists, pp. 340–43. Washington, D.C.

    1917b   Culture and ethnology. New York, Boni & Liveright.

    1920   Primitive society. New York, Boni & Liveright.

    1930   The Omaha and Crow kinship terminologies. Proceedings of the XXIV International Congress of Americanists, pp. 102–8. Hamburg.

    1936   Lewis H. Morgan in historical perspective. *In* Essays in anthropology presented to A. L. Kroeber, pp. 169–81. Berkeley, University of California Press.

    1954   Indians of the Plains. American Museum of

Natural History, Anthropological Handbook no. 1. New York, McGraw Hill Book Co.

MACNEISH, R. S.
1964   Ancient Mesoamerican civilization. Science 143, no. 3606: 531–37.

MANDELBAUM, D.
1940   The Plains Cree. American Museum of Natural History, Anthropological Papers, vol. 37, part 2. New York.

MATHEWS, G. H.
1959   Proto-Siouan kinship terminology. American Anthropologist 61: 252–78.

MORGAN, L. H.
1851   League of the Hode-no-sau-nee, or Iroquois. Rochester, Sage and Brother, Publishers. (Reprinted as League of the Iroquois, with Introd. by William N. Fenton. New York, Corinth Books, 1962.)
1869   Indian migrations. North American Review 109: 391–442.
1871   Systems of consanguinity and affinity of the human family. Smithsonian Contributions to Knowledge, vol. 17. Washington, D.C.
1876   Hue-and-Cry against the Indians. Nation 23: 40–41.
1876   Factory system for Indian reservations. Nation 23: 58–59.
1877   Ancient society. New York, Henry Holt & Co.
1878   The Indian question. Nation 27: 332–33.
1959   The Indian journals, 1859–62. Ed. with Introd. by Leslie A. White. Ann Arbor, University of Michigan Press.

MURDOCK, G. P.
1949   Social structure. New York, Macmillan.
1951   Review of Fred Eggan, Social organization of the western Pueblos. American Anthropologist 53: 250–51.
1955   North American social organization. Davidson Journal of Anthropology (University of Washington) 1, no. 2: 85–97.

NEWMAN, S.
1964   Comparison of Zuni and California Penutian. International Journal of American Linguistics 30, no. 1: 1–13.

OLIVER, S. C.
1962   Ecology and cultural continuity as contributing factors in the social organization of the Plains Indians. Berkeley, University of California Press.

ORTIZ, A.
1965   Dual organization as an operational concept in The Pueblo Southwest. Ethnology 4: 389–96.

QUIMBY, G., JR.
1940   Some notes on kinship and kinship terminology among the Potawatomi of the Huron. Papers of the Michigan Academy of Sciences, Arts, and Letters, vol. 25, 1939 (published 1940). Ann Arbor, Mich.
1960   Indian life in the Upper Great Lakes, 11,000 B.C. to A.D. 1800. Chicago, University of Chicago Press.

RADCLIFFE-BROWN, A. R.
1931   Social organization of Australian tribes. "Oceania" Monographs, no. 1. Melbourne.
1935   Patrilineal and matrilineal succession. Iowa Law Review 20, no. 2.

RESEK, CARL
1960   Louis Henry Morgan: American scholar. Chicago, University of Chicago Press.

RIVERS, W. H. R.
1914   Kinship and social organization. London, Constable & Co. Ltd.

SCHEFFLER, H.
1958   Social change on the northeastern Prairie (The Turtle Mountain Ojibwa). Manuscript in possession of the author.

SCHMITT, KARL and IVA
1952   Wichita kinship, past and present. Norman, University of Oklahoma Book Exchange.

SPECK, F. G.
1909   Ethnology of the Yuchi Indians. University of

Pennsylvania Museum Anthropological Publications, vol. 1. Philadelphia.

1939   Eggan's Yuchi kinship interpretations. American Anthropologist 41: 171–72.

SPICER, E. H.

1962   Cycles of conquest. Tucson, University of Arizona Press.

SPICER, E. H. (ed.)

1961   Perspectives in American Indian cultural change. Chicago, University of Chicago Press.

SPIER, L.

1925   The distribution of kinship systems in North America. University of Washington Publications in Anthropology, vol. 1, no. 2: 71–88.

SPOEHR, A.

1941   Camp, clan and kin among the Cow Creek Seminole of Florida. Field Museum of Natural History, Anthropological Series, vol. 33, no. 1: 1–27, Chicago.

1942   Kinship systems of the Seminole. *Ibid.* vol. 33, no. 2: 31–113.

1944   The Florida Seminole camp. *Ibid.* vol. 33, no. 3: 119–150.

1947   Changing kinship systems. *Ibid.* vol. 33, no. 4: 155–235.

1950   Observations on the study of kinship. American Anthropologist 52: 1–15.

STEWARD, J.

1937   Ecological aspects of southwestern society. Anthropos 32: 87–104.

1938   Basin-Plateau aboriginal sociopolitical groups. Bureau of American Ethnology, Bulletin 120. Washington, D.C.

1955   Theory of cultural change. Urbana, University of Illinois Press.

STRONG, W. D.

1929   Cross-cousin marriage and the culture of the northeast Algonkian. American Anthropologist 31: 777–88.

1935   An introduction to Nebraska archeology. Smithsonian Miscellaneous Collections, vol. 93, no. 10.

1940   From history to prehistory in the northern Great

Plains. *In* Essays in historical anthropology of North America. Smithsonian Miscellaneous Collections, vol. 100, pp. 353–94. Washington, D.C.

SWANTON, J. R.
1905   The social organization of American tribes. American Anthropologist 7: 663–73.

1928   Social organization and social usages of the Indians of the Creek Confederacy. Bureau of American Ethnology, Bulletin 42. Washington, D.C.

1931   Source material for the social and ceremonial life of the Choctaw Indians. Bureau of American Ethnology, Bulletin 103. Washington, D.C.

1946   Indians of the southeastern United States. Bureau of American Ethnology, Bulletin 137. Washington, D.C.

SWANTON, J. R. (ed.)
1932   Rev. John Edwards' account of the Choctaw Indians in the middle of the nineteenth century. Chronicles of Oklahoma, vol. x, no. 3, Oklahoma City, pp. 392–425.

TASK FORCE on INDIAN AFFAIRS
1961   Report to the Secretary of the Interior by the Task Force on Indian Affairs (mimeographed).

TAX, SOL
1955   From Lafitau to Radcliffe-Brown: a short history of the study of social organization. *In* Social anthropology of North American tribes, ed. F. Eggan, pp. 445–81. Enlarged edition. Chicago, University of Chicago Press.

TYLOR, E. B.
1871   Primitive culture. 2 vols. London.
1889   On a method of investigating the development of institutions, applied to laws of marriage and descent. Journal of the Royal Anthropological Institute 18: 245–69.

WAGNER, G.
n.d.   Personal communication with regard to Yuchi kinship terminology, 1933.

WALLACE, A. F. C.
1961   Cultural composition of the Handsome Lake

religion. *In* Symposium on Cherokee and Iroquois culture, ed. W. N. Fenton and J. Gulick. Bureau of American Ethnology, Bulletin 180. Washington, D.C.

WALLACE, E., and E. A. HOEBEL
1952   The Comanches, lords of the southern Plains. Norman, University of Oklahoma Press.

WAUCHOPE, R., *et al.*
1956   Seminars in archeology: 1955. Memoirs of the Society for American Archeology, no. 11. Salt Lake City.

WEDEL, W.
1961   Prehistoric man on the Great Plains. Norman, University of Oklahoma Press.
1963   The High Plains and their utilization by the Indian. American Antiquity 29, no. 1: 1–16.

WELTFISH, G.
1965   The lost universe. New York. Basic Books, Inc.

WHITE, L. A.
1948   Lewis H. Morgan: Pioneer in the theory of social evolution. *In* An introduction to the history of sociology, ed. H. E. Barnes, pp. 138–54. Chicago, University of Chicago Press.

WHITE, L. A. (ed.)
1959   Lewis Henry Morgan, the Indian journals, 1859–62. Ann Arbor, University of Michigan Press.

WILLIS, W. S., JR.
1963   Patrilineal institutions in southeastern North America. Ethnohistory 10, no. 3: 250–69.

WILSON, E.
1959   Apologies to the Iroquois. New York, Farrar, Strauss and Cudahy.

WISSLER, C.
1917   The American Indian. 1st ed. New York.
1922   The American Indian. 2d ed. New York.

WITTFOGEL, K. A., and E. S. GOLDFRANK
1943   Some aspects of Pueblo mythology and society. Journal of American Folklore 56: 17-30.

INDEX